Great British Families

LEGENDS AND TRADITIONS

By the same author

Britain's Haunted Heritage
Ghosts of Wessex
Historic Heraldic Families
The Two Beaux
Unfamiliar Spirits

Great British Families

Legends and Traditions

Keith B. Poole

ROBERT HALE · LONDON

First published in Great Britain 1992

ISBN 0 7090 4346 5

Robert Hale Limited
Clerkenwell House
Clerkenwell Green
London EC1R 0HT

Photoset in North Wales by
Derek Doyle & Associates, Mold, Clwyd.
Printed in Great Britain by
St Edmundsbury Press Ltd., Bury St Edmunds, Suffolk.
Bound by WBC Bookbinders Ltd, Bridgend, Glamorgan.

Contents

For Madeline

Illustrations

Between pages 96 and 97

PICTURE CREDITS

All illustrations by Madeline Poole, with the exception of the *Luck of Muncaster*, courtesy of Muncaster Castle Estate Office.

Acknowledgements

I am indebted to the Court of the Company of Watermen & Lightermen for granting me permission to include an account of the annual ceremony of the presentation of the Knollys Rose; my grateful thanks also to Suzanne Lofthouse, Personal Assistant to the Lord Mayor of the City of London. I must also express thanks to Guildhall Library, London for much help in my researches and information about other traditional ceremonies; to David Watkins, Administration Manager of the National Westminster Bank (Stuckey's branch) Bath, for permission to photograph the splendid wood-carving of the bust of Bladud, once king of Bath. I acknowledge much help from Peter Bamford, Alec Rogers, Harold Leach, and the Muncaster Castle Estate office. I owe an immense debt to the countless libraries and historians of local folklore studies and events in the United Kingdom, notably Chester, Newcastle upon Tyne, Fowey and Hertford. To my wife, in her capacity as my right hand throughout the compilation of this book, my inexpressible gratitude for her patience, meticulous checking of my manuscript, taping and recording very many essential documents for research, all of which has made the writing of my book possible.

Introduction

All legends are based on historical truth and every family in this book has had one or more member who became legendary, many of them emerging as widely accepted historic folk heroes. In both history and legend, the story of these families is founded on their personal traditions and ceremonies, the vicissitudes which befell them, the supposed power of curses that caused some of them to die out, the privileges and honours awarded them. In the case of those families bearing coats of arms, the heraldic imagery of giants, dragons, fabulous beasts and other animals, often adds meaning to the family's traditions and legends.

The world of legend is an integral part of all folklore; two or three different nations will often have similar legends springing from the same original idea. Ascetics and scholars may not accept the existence of giants, dragons, saints and fairies, but wonderful evidence of their existence is given in a number of stories in this book. Those families who possess such traditions are rightly proud of them, and it may well be that these traditions are founded on historical fact.

The proudest of all the family traditions are those concerning feudal tenures of manors, special duties such as holding the rope of the ship carrying a queen abroad; the annual presentation of a red rose to the sovereign when travelling through Hungerford in Berkshire, a rent first established by John of Gaunt; the beautiful ceremony of the presentation made annually to the Lord Mayor of London, in payment of rent by the Knollys family centuries ago; another rent of a red-footed falcon paid by a Scottish nobleman; or the ceremony of the presentation of a falchion by the Durham families of Conyers and Pollard. These are true legends, not myths

The days of the wandering story-tellers of centuries ago are legends in themselves. They travelled across the countryside, particularly in Wales, searching for rich patrons who would offer hospitality and festive board to them. Everyone would assemble in torch-lit halls to enjoy hours, even days, of story-telling by men who must have had prodigious memories and gift of speech.

Perhaps the best description of the word legend is by C.V. Wedgwood in her book *William the Silent*, when she says 'Legend is often a symbolic rendering of a whole atmosphere.' What could be more atmospheric than that created by these story-tellers in the torch-lit halls of their patrons in those far off days? I myself have heard many such stories under the palm-trees of Egypt and Arabia, in cottages on the Isle of Mull, where the listeners sat spellbound by the wonderful tales they heard, being transported to a different world. When these stories first appeared in manuscript and then in print at the beginning of the fifteenth century, the story-tellers ceased to be in demand. The legends became a wonderful world of their own, medieval masterpieces of great skill and beauty which have survived down to the present day. No one has summarized the word legend with such understanding and affection as Sir Winston Churchill in his *History of the English-speaking People*. He wrote: 'We should find ourselves in the presence of a theme as well founded as inspired, and as inalienable as the inheritance of mankind as the *Odyssey* or the Old Testament. It is all true, or it ought to be, and more and better besides.'

1 *Family Legends*

THE BLADUDS

THE SWINEHERD PRINCE

For centuries millions of people have visited the Roman baths in the city of Bath, believing that they were founded by the Romans. Only those who see the statue in the niche behind the King's Bath and read the citation beneath it, have evidence of the true founder. It reads:

> BLADUD son to Lud Hudibras the Eighth King of the Britons, A great Philosopher and Mathematician bred at Athens And recorded the First Discoverer and Founder of these Bathes Eight Hundred and Sixty Three yeares Before Christ that is Two Thousand Five Hundred thirty Five Years SINCE ANNO DOMINI 1672.

The whole life of this remarkable character has become traditional. His father, King Lud Hudibras, claimed direct descent from King Brutus, the legendary founder of Britain, as recorded by the twelfth-century chronicler Geoffrey of Monmouth. The king held court in his palace near Stonehenge in Wiltshire. From quite an early age Prince Bladud revealed considerable talents. He was modest, very good-looking and popular with his father's subjects. Tragedy, however, suddenly threatened not only his own life but the lives of everyone at court when a white spot, the sign of the dreaded leprosy, appeared on his face. His father had no option but to banish him, in spite of the tears and pleadings of the prince's mother. Before he left she gave him a gold ring suspended from a gold chain which she placed round his neck. She told him that if ever he became cured of the disease, he was to return to court, and produce the ring as proof that he was her son and heir to his father's throne. The parting must have been bitter indeed for both knew there was no real hope of recovery.

He had nothing of value, and only countless acres of forest land in which to hide, with little prospect of finding any work. He had only fruit and wild berries for food and was in considerable danger from wild animals as he began his wanderings. After a day or so, however, he reached a swineherd's hovel where he begged for food, shelter and work to pay for them. The swineherd, if puzzled at the request from such a handsome young man, took pity on him without any questions and gave him food and shelter. The next morning he was put in charge of a herd of swine, told not to let them wander off and to return with them before nightfall.

As there were acorns everywhere on which the pigs could gorge, there was no problem to begin with, but it was harder to keep them together. Towards the late afternoon, however, Bladud saw with horror that one of the pigs had the same white spot as himself. He must have given the disease to the animal when he touched it. As they jostled and pushed each other in their greed for acorns he saw others with the white spot. He was terrified, knowing now that he dared not go back to the swineherd. It was easier to drive them on rather than return as he had promised. Suddenly he noticed that the pigs had reached a river, hesitating what to do. Bladud at once shouted and urged them on until they plunged in and crossed to the other side. That night they all huddled together, but their constant grunts, even screams, as their bodies itched with the disease, made sleep impossible.

Bladud realized the magnitude of what had happened. He himself was now suffering acutely from the leprosy spreading over his body. He could never even have imagined that the name Swineford given to the crossing place of the pigs is used to this day.

The following days became increasingly anxious for Bladud, though his main fear was that the swineherd should have followed them along the wide tracks they had made through the forest. Suddenly there was a mad stampede of heaving, scrambling pigs which ended dramatically as Bladud, with astonished eyes, saw that they were in a swamp of stinking green slime in which they wallowed with obvious pleasure. When the first one emerged, followed by the others, Bladud saw that the scars they had previously borne on their bodies had gone. They no longer sought acorns, simply rushed in and out of the swamp excitedly. When at last they had had enough, and began to lie exhausted in the sun, Bladud decided he would try the same treatment.

He stripped off all his clothes and rushed into the churned-up water of the swamp, wallowing in it as if in a hot bath. He spent the rest of the day there, emerging just before darkness fell, and saw with wonder that his body was cured of leprosy. The next morning, rounding up the scattered pigs, he led them back along the tracks to the swineherd's hovel and the by now infuriated swineherd. Bladud immediately showed him the gold chain and the ring he wore round his neck, telling him who he was and urging him to sty the pigs and go with him to his father's court, where he would be greatly rewarded for what he had done. On reaching the palace Bladud told the guards who he was, but they disbelieved the ill-clad, dirty-looking strangers and forbade their entrance until Bladud divested himself of his chain and ring, commanding one of the guards to take them immediately to the queen to prove his identity. The day ended with a great feast from his rejoicing parents and all their subjects; as promised the swineherd was amply rewarded.

The prince developed his talents rapidly and was sent to Athens to study mathematics and philosophy, but all the time he was planning what he would do after his father's death. Eleven years later Bladud became king. He at once moved his court to the territory in which the swamp was situated, calling the place Caer Badon and dedicating it to the goddess *Sul*, the Romans later named it *Aquae Sulis* and it is now the city of Bath. Legend states that he sank four tuns, two of glass, full of salt and brimstone, the other two of burning brass. These were placed directly over the swamp for its obvious medicinal qualities, and later became the hot springs of the baths which made the city internationally famous.

Bladud next became deeply interested in necromancy and black magic, and was regarded by his subjects as a wizard. He decided to become the first man to fly in Britain, choosing the hill overlooking the city, known as Solisbury Hill, from which to start the flight. Let Geoffrey of Monmouth relate the result of Bladud's attempt to imitate the efforts of the classical Daedalus:

> ... a very ingenious Man and taught Necromancy in his Kingdom, nor left off pursuing his Magical Operations, till he attempted to fly to the upper Region of the Air with Wings he had prepared, and fell down upon the Temple of *Apollo* in the city ... where he was dashed to Pieces.

Wise as Bladud undoubtedly was he could never even have imagined that the curative quality of his hot springs would become known world-wide. There is regrettably no record of his burial-place, but he left one son named Lear who, according to Geoffrey of Monmouth, gave rise to an even more astonishing legend. He founded the city of Leicester, reigned for sixty years, but had no male issue, only three daughters named Regan, Goneril and Cordelia. At what point Shakespeare discovered the story will never be known but he wrote, in his *King Lear*, one of the greatest historical dramas in the English language.

Geoffrey of Monmouth relates that Cordelia buried her father in a certain vault under the river Soar upon which he had founded the city of Leicester which he had built to the honour of the God Janus. 'And here all the Workmen of the City, upon the anniversary Solemnity of that Festival, used to begin their yearly Labours.' Cordelia ruled for five years before her sisters rose in rebellion and imprisoned her, when she took her own life. Geoffrey of Monmouth became widely known for his history, his stories were retold by other chroniclers over and over again. It would therefore seem that there is much truth in the legend of Bladud and his descendants.

The name of Bladud is still prominent in the city of Bath, notably in Bladud Buildings attached to the Paragon, where in 1790 Bladud Bank opened its premises at no. 2. Through a series of amalgamations over the years, the building gives the National Westminster Bank its oldest association in the city. A model of the head of King Bladud, reputedly carved by Grinling Gibbons, one of the finest wood-carvers in England and a friend of Sir Christopher Wren, is also possessed by the bank. It is in contemporary style, and since the bust has a Van Dyck beard as well as a lace collar it in no way resembles the figure of King Bladud in the King's Bath. It used to stand on a plinth before work was done in the Banking Hall. It is the intention of the bank to have the bust cleaned and exhibited in a more prominent place so that the public can see this fine carving of a legendary great king; one whose discovery was to make Bath famous throughout the whole world, and attract millions of tourists to the city.

THE CLIFFORDS

FAIR ROSAMUND

Two years after the death of Henry II in 1189, St Hugh of Avalon, the formidable Bishop of Lincoln whom the king had brought from Burgundy, visited Godstow Nunnery in Oxfordshire, in whose diocese it then was. There, preceded by the abbess and her nuns he entered the chapel where his horrified eyes saw in the middle of the choir and before the high altar a large tomb. It was covered with a white silk pall adorned with flowers within a circle of tall and brightly burning wax candles.

'Who is buried here in such state?' the bishop demanded of the abbess.

'It is the fair Rosamund whom King Henry so dearly loved and for whose sake he has been such a munificent benefactor to this poor house', she answered.

'Then take out of this place the harlot and bury her outside the church so that other women may be frightened from keeping adulterous company with men', the angry bishop commanded.

Compelled to obey the outraged bishop's orders for fear of the dreaded penalty of excommunication, the abbess instructed the nuns to destroy the tomb. They, however, in disobedience and secrecy, first removed Rosamund's bones, which they placed in a heavily perfumed leather bag and later reluctantly interred in a second tomb built in the cemetery outside the church, where it remained until it was destroyed three centuries later.

The story of fair Rosamund, the beautiful, gentle and dearly beloved mistress of Henry II is an immortal one, shining out of the dark pages of medieval English history like a bright flame; created out of legends, poetry, ballads and chapbooks. No historical facts concerning her life survive, not even the exact dates of her birth or death, nor where and how she died, nor for how long she and the king were lovers. Historians and chroniclers are totally at variance, disputing whether the manner of her death was by brutal torture, by the slashing of her veins in a hot bath, or by poison. Only in acceptance of her singular beauty, her gentle nature, and her love for the king do they agree. Of all the great scholars and chroniclers in the court of Henry II, including such men as Giraldus Cambrensis (Gerald the Welshman) and Peter of Blois, only the first is harsh about her very name, saying that it was not *Rosa Mundi* (Rose of the World) but *Rosa Immundi* or Unchaste Rose, with which the bishop obviously agreed when he ordered the destruction of her tomb.

Indeed, it is surprising that no more has come down to us from these contemporary chroniclers, since their descriptions of the king himself and his court are so meticulous and so vivid that they seem as fresh today as when they were first written in Latin eight centuries ago. To these men gossip was their life-blood; scandals, intrigues, pastimes, passions, all were tasted with the same relish they had from the wines they drank. Of them all Walter Map has left the most vivid account of those times, yet he is strangely silent about Rosamund.

The brief, passionate and tragic love-story of the king and his mistress is as old as time, that of a desperately unhappy, disillusioned and embittered husband whose marriage to a vindictive, dominant and scorned wife (whom he finally imprisoned) lay in ruins. In Rosamund he found the love, understanding and affection he so desperately needed. He had had many concubines in his life, yet none save Rosamund has come down through history to us, for her legend is an imperishable one.

Rosamund bore Henry a son, William Longespee, later created Earl of Salisbury by the king. He died in 1226 and was the first person to be buried in Salisbury Cathedral. The tomb is of wood and his stone effigy the finest in the cathedral. He lies in mail armour holding a shield on his left side adorned with six golden lions on a blue base; traces of these colours are still visible after eight centuries.

Rosamund was the daughter of Walter de Clifford who came over to England with William the Conqueror and changed his original name of Fitzponce after obtaining Clifford Castle in Herefordshire, still marked on the Ordnance Survey map. This illustrious family is still extant in the Cliffords of Chudleigh in Devon, whose house, Ugbrooke, though a private home, is open to the public during the summer months.

In 1299 Robert de Clifford was summoned to Parliament as 1st Baron. They fought with distinction for the Lancastrian cause during the Wars of the Roses, and became ennobled when Henry, 11th Baron, was created Earl of Cumberland. One of the most remarkable women in their history was Lady Anne, his daughter, who inherited all her father's eccentricities and vast estates. She was married twice, both times unhappily. Lady Anne inherited no fewer than six castles, living in turn in one or other of them, and was engaged in a feud with her uncle, the 4th Earl, which lasted for thirty-eight years. This bitter internecine war over the possession of the Barony of Skipton finally resulted in victory for Lady Anne, for she outlived her uncle the 4th Earl. A 'Lady Anne Clifford Trail' is now being promoted to mark the 400th anniversary of the birth of the woman who enriched the Yorkshire Dales and Eden Valley with twenty-six years of restoring and building castles and churches.

When or where King Henry first met Rosamund and fell deeply in love with her is not certain, but Furley in his *History of the Weald of Kent* states that her home is traditionally associated with Osthanger Castle in Kent: 'Two of the localities in this ancient castle were named after her. One was the 160-foot-long upper room named Rosamund's Gallery; the other was a tower flanking the castle walls called Rosamund's Tower.' This was in fact a medieval dovecote containing shelves for many hundreds of birds for food in times of siege or famine. It seems probable, however, that he met her through her father. He was not only one of the royal courtiers in attendance on the king at Woodstock near Oxford, but also a great benefactor of Godstow Nunnery, not far away, where Rosamund was educated.

Since so much of Rosamund's life story is both fragmentary and legendary, it cannot be proved that she was hidden in Osthanger Castle, however, her presence at Woodstock is far more certain. There, according to the chronicler Higden, she was secreted 'in a house of wonderful working so that no man or woman might come to her but he that was instructed by the king or such as were right secret with him touching the matter. The house after some was named Labyrinthus or Daedelus' work which was wrought like a knot in the garden called a Maze'. Another chronicler said that under the maze Henry had built vaults with stone-and-brick arches; this was proved, he wrote, by the fact that a certain part of the park had a hollow ring when walked on. After Rosamund's death, and indeed for some 500 more years, the place became known as Rosamund's Bower, and all the rubble gathered there was finally removed by order of the ruthless Sarah, Duchess of Marlborough, to help build Blenheim Palace.

In spite of all this secrecy rumours were soon circulating the court about the king and Rosamund, and the person most deeply hurt was her father, Walter de Clifford. He, however, was powerless to defend her for fear of arousing the king's anger. But such was Henry's love for her that, according to yet another chronicler 'he at once provided her with everything she desired'. Soon Henry himself became less secretive and even began to flaunt Rosamund's name abroad as his beloved mistress, a woman whose beauty and nature were ethereal. It was therefore natural that the news at last reached the imprisoned Queen Eleanor at Winchester. All her rancour, hatred, bitterness and jealousy festered within her as she sought some way of destroying Henry through Rosamund.

In order to do this Eleanor had first to dispose of

Rosamund. Her only chance of revenge came when, as occasionally happened, Henry held a full court at Woodstock to which she was brought from Winchester under close guard by the king's judiciar. She attended the court as a mere figurehead, rather than as the rightful queen, for the ever-suspicious Henry granted her no freedom. With all the guile, cunning and intense hatred of a scorned woman, Eleanor waited for the slightest chance of discovering Rosamund's secret bower. When at last the moment came is not recorded, nor is it known how she managed to escape her constant guards – unless it was by bribery, so easily managed in those days. It is agreed by several authorities, however, that one of Henry's spurs was brought to her on his return from a day's hunting and there her eager eyes saw, wound round it, part of a silken coloured thread. It was all she needed. Shortly after, whilst walking in the park, her searching eyes saw, leading away through the grass, the guideline of the coloured silken thread. The rest was easy, could she but bribe her guard.

This also she managed to do and following the winding thread came first to a secret hidden door below the park, then to a second door which she triumphantly burst open to confront the terrified Rosamund. The method by which Eleanor murdered Rosamund is not certain; some say she was killed with a dagger, others that her wrists were slashed by two old crones who forcibly held her down in a bath of water, or that she was poisoned. Poison seems most likely since the shape of a cup was figured on her tomb and was later the subject of a ballad on Rosamund's death.

> And casting up her eyes to heaven
> She did for mercy call
> And drinking up the poison strong
> Her life she lost withal.

And when that death through every limb
Had shown its greatest spite
Her chiefest foes did plain confess
She was a glorious wight.

Henry gave her a funeral befitting a queen, and on her last journey from Woodstock to Godstow Nunnery, the king had a cross erected at each spot where her coffin rested. A century later Henry's descendant Edward I carried out the same homage to his wife, Eleanor of Castile, on her last journey to Westminster Abbey. All the Rosamund crosses have disappeared, the last to survive was the one near the Lower Wolvercote Toll Bridge. In majestic state and splendour, amid incense and chanting, Rosamund was laid to rest in that stately and magnificent tomb the irate and indignant Bishop of Lincoln later ordered to be destroyed.

The second tomb erected by the unhappy and mourning nuns beyond the precincts, remained for three-and-a-half centuries until the dissolution of the monasteries by Henry VIII, when the tomb was broken up. But just before its destruction it was seen by Thomas Allen, aged ninety, of Gloster Hall, now Worcester College, or by an eyewitness who had told him the following story.

Amidst the broken fragments was one bearing the words 'Tumba Rosamundae' and another bearing the final carved insult from Eleanor's son, John, later King John, inscribed in stone after his father's death. They were in Latin, which translated, reads:

Here lies entombed the World's Rose,
Not fragrant now but stinking, she who used to used to smell so sweet.

The story of the epitaph cut into one of the side slabs of the tomb has been repeated by antiquaries from Hearne to Anthony Wood: 'Upon which were interchangeable weavings drawn out, decked with roses red and green, and the picture of the cup out of which she drank the poison given her by the Queen carved in stone'.

Henry had died, Eleanor was released from prison by her sons to continue until her death a life of strife and constant warfare. By sheer irony surely and not by choice, her body was laid to rest in the abbey of Fontevraud in the same vault as the husband she had hated as much as he hated her.

Rosamund's tomb has vanished forever, her secret bower at Woodstock is no more, yet the legend lingers on as if she died but a short time ago and not eight centuries. Perhaps the the most beautiful quality of the whole story is captured by the simple words of John Leland who wrote at the time of the breaking-up of her tomb: 'Her bones were inclosed in lead, and inside the lead in leather. When it was opened a very sweet smell came out of it'.

THE DRAKES

THE DRUM

Every nation has its own undefeated and undying heroes round whom countless legends and traditions have gathered over the centuries. England and Wales have King Arthur, 'the once and future king', Hereward the Wake, Lord Nelson and Sir Francis Drake. In every case there is a firm belief that these heroes are immortal, only sleeping somewhere ready to return at the least sign of danger to their country. The many legends concerning Sir Francis Drake are an integral part of the folklore of Devon where he was born, beloved especially by the citizens of Plymouth.

The Drake family lived as poor, hard-working farmers in Crowndale, near Tavistock. Francis, their first child was born *c.*1540, though opinions differ widely on the exact year. They were devout Protestants, living quietly and unobtrusively, until their lives were shattered by the 1549 Catholic uprising in Devon against the Cranmer prayer-book. The Drake family and others were driven from their homes and farms and forced to flee for their lives to the Island, now known as Drake's Island. There they took refuge until King Edward VI's ships took them off and carried them to Kent, where, on the Medway, they found an old hulk which became their home, surrounded by ships of the first modern navy. Drake's bitter, lasting hate of Catholics began.

Years later his great-nephew wrote of this part of their life:

> ... in the hulk of that ship wherein many of his younger sons were born. He had twelve in all and as it pleased God to give most of them a being upon water, so the greatest part of them died at sea. The youngest, who thought he went as far as any, yet died at home, whose posterity inherits that which by himself and this noble gentleman, the old brother, was hardly yet worthily gotten.

The years were hard indeed for the young Francis, exchanging farm-labouring for working on ships. He was greatly helped by his Plymouth cousin John Hawkins, some eight years older than himself, later the famous sea captain Sir John Hawkins and already rich from slave-trading. Drake, who sailed twice to the West Indies with him, had no liking for slave-trading but his quick mind coveted the wealth of the Spanish Main for himself.

Thus it was that after making two such voyages, and at thirty-two years of age, on Whitsunday 24 May 1572, Captain Drake set sail from Plymouth in the *Pascha*, 70 tons, with his brother John in the *Swan*, 25 tons, and with seventy-three volunteers from Plymouth embarked for the West Indies on a daring voyage. One year later, on a Sunday morning, he anchored in Plymouth Sound with considerable treasure aboard. The news of his arrival travelled like fire through the city even reaching St Andrew's church causing the whole congregation to rush out leaving the astounded preacher in his pulpit in the middle of a sermon. From that day to this he has been Plymouth's greatest hero.

His popularity grew beyond bounds when in 1577/80 he became the first Englishman to circumnavigate the world in his great ship the *Golden Hind*. In 1581, Queen Elizabeth I made a rare visit to Deptford to knight him on his own ship.

It was not only his naval achievements that astonished the people of Devon but the legends that began to grow about him. It was said that he communed with the Devil; that he practised magic; that he was called by the Spaniards, who now hated him, *El Draque*, the Dragon; that he was a wizard.

The citizens became even more convinced that he had strange powers when he offered to bring fresh water to Plymouth at a time of desperate shortage. Drake set out on horseback, and somewhere on the moors he at last found a source of clear, pure water. After uttering some words of magic, he then rode back and legend says that the stream followed him to the city. Known today as the Burrator reservoir, the place is visited by countless people. The miracle is commemorated on an etched plate, the gift of the water company.

Another commemoration of Drake's gift of water is carried out in a remarkable ceremony known as 'Fyshynge Feaste' held in June or July when the Mayor and the Plymouth City Council go up to Burrator reservoir and enjoy a lunch of grilled lake trout. They meet on the lawn by the head weir where:

> The Party being assembled on the lawn a Goblet of Pure Water taken on the Weir by the Corporation Surveyor is handed by him to the Chairman of the Water Committee who presents the same to the Mayor and requests him to

> drink thereof; 'To the pious Memory of Sir Francis Drake', and passing the Cup from one to the other, each drinks and repeats the same words. Another Goblet being filled with Wine is then presented by the Chamberlain to the Mayor, who drinks the toast: 'May the descendants of him who brought the Water never want Wine.'

This great gift of Sir Francis Drake was cherished by the Plymouth people. Concerned that the working of the tin-mines on the moors might pollute the pure water, they caused the Corporation to authorize regular inspections of the reservoir and the stream.

In 1582 Drake was elected Mayor of Plymouth and became MP for Bossiney, but he was saddened by the death of his first wife. He next bought Buckland Abbey from Sir Richard Grenville of the *Revenge,* now in the possession of the National Trust. An extremely rich man and perhaps tired of absences and voyages at sea he married for a second time. She was the very beautiful Elizabeth Sydenham, the only surviving daughter of Sir George Sydenham of Combe Sydenham Hall, Monksilver in Somerset. It was she who became the principal of one of the most persistent and most dubious of all Somerset and Devon legends. There are at least three versions of the story.

Elizabeth was said to have been so depressed by the seven years of sea voyages without news of Drake that her parents were constantly urging her to remarry as they were convinced of his death. Finally, she accepted the proposal of another man. One story says that as she was entering the church of the wedding a cannonball crashed down on to the train of her dress. Another that she was actually standing at the altar when a cannonball crashed down between her and her groom. Another that she was in her own home, Combe Sydenham Hall, when the cannonball crashed between her and her groom. In each story she was said to have cried out: 'I am still a wife' and broken off the marriage at once.

First of all, one should note that Drake was never absent at sea for seven years, his longest voyage was that of three years circumnavigating the world. The most dubious part of this legend concerns Drake himself who, on being informed that his wife was to remarry, at once fired a cannonball under the sea from somewhere on the Spanish Main. The cannonball travelled under the globe to land in Somerset and Drake appeared next day to claim Elizabeth. The cannonball is to be seen today in Combe Sydenham Hall where legend has it that if it is ever removed it will roll itself back again. The house is open to the public at certain times. Elizabeth's portrait may be seen, as well as many other Drake relics, including the celebrated drum in the Drake Gallery of Buckland Abbey.

For some years Sir Francis lived quietly at Buckland Abbey, during which time he planned his attack on Cadiz 'to singe the King of Spain's beard' in 1587. One year later he set out from Plymouth as vice-admiral to help defeat the Armada. Once again, tales of his wizardry begat a fresh legend. It was while he was playing his celebrated game of bowls (in fact, kales – a form of skittles rather than bowls) that he was informed that the Spanish Armada had been sighted, an immortal story in every English history book. Undisturbed by the news, Sir Francis quietly finished his game then demanded that a large block of timber and a hatchet should be brought to him. He cut the timber into short logs, and threw each one into the Sound, uttering words of magic, where upon they all became fully rigged and armed ships, and were sent out as fireships to attack and sink the Spanish fleet.

In the year 1595 Drake set out once again for the Spanish Main, together with his cousin Sir John Hawkins. The voyage was to end in complete disaster when they found themselves outmanoeuvred by the watchful Spanish fleet. Worse came when disease claimed the life of Sir John Hawkins and later caused the death of Drake himself. On 27 January 1596, Drake lay dying at Puerto

Bello in the Caribbean where he was buried at sea. His last wish and command was that his drum, which had travelled with him round the world, should be sent back to his Devon home, Buckland Abbey, where it lies to this very day in the Gallery named after him. Drake said that if ever England was in trouble and danger he would hear the drumbeats, even in Paradise, and would come to the aid of his country.

Of all the many legends concerning Drake's drum, the following is surely the strangest. For many years, the Devonians refused to believe in Drake's death. Rumours of drumbeats ran round the West Country from time to time, but never more than at the end of the First World War when, in 1919, the German Fleet surrendered at Scapa Flow. A single drumbeat was heard on the flagship of the Grand Fleet as their ships closed round the Germans. Commands were at once issued to all British ships to find the drummer responsible for the unauthorised drum roll.

Every sailor was found to be at his appointed station and the mystery was never solved. Those sailors familiar with the Drake legend were convinced that it was Drake's drum, that he had been with them all through the war and had brought his country to victory.

Drake had no children so Buckland passed to his brother Thomas whose son, another Francis, was created a baronet by James I in 1622. The 5th Baronet, another Sir Francis, died unmarried in 1794 and the Baronetcy became extinct. Their coat of arms was a black shield with a fess between two silver stars, the Pole Star and the Southern Cross, both seen by Sir Francis Drake on his historic circumnavigation of the globe.

THE FITZWARYNS

DICK WHITTINGTON

Few families have made a more dramatic entry into history than the Fitzwaryns, Fitzwarines, or Fitzwarrens (as they have been variously called). They came from Normandy to England with William the Conqueror in 1066. The first of them was given command of the Marches, towards the rebellious Welsh but distinguished himself at once by entering the tournament lists contending for the prize of a bride, Mallet the daughter of the Lord of Whittington Castle in Shropshire. She was beautiful and brought a large dowry to her marriage. Little did he know that the name of his family would become associated not so much with his military skill and courage, a tradition continued by successive heirs, as with an immortal legend, that of Dick Whittington, his cat and Hugh Fitzwarren's daughter Alice who married Richard Whittington during the reign of Richard II.

The story of a poor boy running away from home to a great city – London – believing that the streets are paved with gold, has been repeated over the centuries in some thirty countries, as far afield as Egypt, Persia (now Iran) and India. First told in England, the legend has delighted millions of people, children and adults, through the centuries, in annual pantomimes. Dick Whittington and his cat have become an integral part of the folklore history of our country. If, since legends are unauthenticated, stories handed down by tradition are popularly regarded as historical, then Dick Whittington is no exception. Historians have disputed among themselves ever since as to who really was thrice Lord Mayor of London.

Gloucestershire makes a convincing claim that he was born in that county and is proud that he was one of their greatest citizens. There is no doubt at all that there was a Richard Whittington, the third son of Sir William Whittington of Paunley and his wife Joan. She was the daughter of the High Sheriff of Gloucester and the widow of Thomas Berkeley of Cobberley, Gloucestershire. As he married her 'without licence' he was outlawed by the Crown and could not be redeemed except by payment of a huge fine which might have spelt bankruptcy. In those times, of course, it was only the heir to a title and estate who was of any real consequence, the rule of primogeniture meant that a second son, let alone a third, as Richard was, received nothing. In this history, Richard would have left for London to find a job, later married a rich woman, become first a Sheriff and then Lord Mayor of London, and held that high office three times.

That fine historian John Stow, in his *Survey of London* published in 1598, only partly confirms the claims of Gloucestershire, but most importantly gives the name of Hugh Fitzwarren, whose daughter Alice married Richard Whittington. He tells us that a Richard Whittington, Mercer, built almshouses for thirteen poor men and a tutor, the former to receive thirteen pence a week and the latter sixteen pence weekly in perpetuity. He goes on:

> ... These were bound to pray for the good estate of Richard Whitington and Alice his wife their founders, and for Sir William Whitington, knight, and for Dame Joan his wife, and for Hugh Fitzwaren and Dame Molde his wife, the fathers and mothers of the said Richard Whitington and Alice his wife, for King Richard II and Thomas of Woodstocke, Duke of Glocester, special lords and promoters of the said Richard Whitington etc. The licence for this foundation was granted by King Henry IV., the 11th of his reign, and in the 12th of the same king's reign the Mayor and commonalty of London granted to Richard Whitington a vacant piece of ground, thereon to build his college in the Royall, all of which was confirmed by Henry VI., the 3rd of his reign ...

He then tells us how Richard Whittington was buried three times in the church of St Michael de Pater Noster Royall (burned down in the Great Fire of London), each time by orders of the Crown who thought he had been buried with much treasure, but none being found they stripped his body of its leaden sheath.

Now whilst all these facts are historical, for there was a Sir Richard Whittington who was thrice Lord Mayor of London in 1397, 1406 and 1419, there is no evidence whatsoever of a Mr Hugh Fitzwarren, Mercer. There is, however, a Sir Ivo Fitzwaryn of Dorset who died in 1423, the year of Richard Whittington's death, leaving a daughter named Alice. However, there is no evidence whether Stow's Dame Molde was the mother of Alice Fitzwarren.

Sir Richard Whittington amassed a very considerable fortune as a mercer. He is said to have paid for the wedding trousseaux of both the daughters of Henry IV and lent huge sums of money to the Crown for the wars against France, including the famous victory of Henry V at Agincourt. Legend has it that Whittington, whilst entertaining Prince Henry to a luncheon in Guildhall and discussing the cost of the wars, suddenly rose, took from his pocket the signed bonds of the loans, and threw them into the fire, releasing the Crown from all debts. The prince at once cried out, 'Never had prince such a subject', to which Whittington replied, 'Never had subject such a prince.'

The least known origin of the legend originates with a certain Mr Hugh Fitzwarren, seemingly claiming descent from the Fitzwaryn family, who was a wealthy merchant living in Leadenhall Street, London. He was one day visited by a very poor, raggedly dressed orphan who said his name was Whittington and he was desperately looking for any job to keep himself alive. Mr Fitzwarren, shocked at the boy's appearance and taking pity on him, sent him down to the kitchen to see the cook, who gave him the job of a scullion and turnspit in the kitchen. It was one of the worst and hardest jobs to which the cook, who did not really want him, added considerable abuse and cruelty.

The boy suffered greatly and would have run away several times were it not for the kindness of the master's daughter Alice.

Dick had bought a cat for one penny to deal with his rat-infested attic, whom he fed with scraps from the kitchen. One day Mr Fitzwarren summoned all his staff to his office to inform them that as a merchant he was sending one of his ships, filled with goods, far away on a voyage that might mean two or three years at sea. It was his custom to invite each one to have a tiny share in its good fortune, however small the contribution. Such offerings he was sure would receive God's blessing on them all. Each of those present offered a coin but Dick had no money and could only offer his most precious possession, his cat. His master, puzzled yet touched by this singular act of generosity, accepted the offer and his ship, *Union*, set sail the next day with the cat on board.

Months passed and life became more and more unbearable for Dick, brutally treated by the cook and terrified by the rats in his attic. At last he ran away from it all, not knowing where he would go. Some ballads say that he first reached Holloway and then Highgate Hill where, exhausted and tired, he sat on a stone. This might have been the remains of a wayside cross or a milestone, but whatever it was it is now encircled by railings and surmounted by the figure of a cat. It was there that he suddenly heard the bells of one of the city churches ringing out (believed to be Bow Bells), which seemed to sing the words,

> Turn again, Whittington,
> Lord Mayor of London.

Without understanding what the words meant, Dick felt himself impelled to return and he found unbelievable good news.

Summoned to Mr Fitzwarren's room, he was sure he would be severely reprimanded or even dismissed for running away. Instead he listened with astonishment as his master told him that when the *Union* had reached a port on the Barbary coast, its captain had been told that the king's palace was overrun with rats. The captain had therefore suggested he could lend him a cat. Though the king had never seen such an animal, he said he would like to try the experiment and accepted the offer of Dick's cat. After a few days the king sent word that he was so delighted with the result that he would exchange the cat for the whole of the ship's cargo. In addition he would give ten times more than the cargo value to keep the cat. The captain naturally agreed so that the extra gold paid was rightly due to Dick. In addition, Mr Fitzwarren said Dick could have anything else that he dearly wished without refusal. Since Dick had never had any kindness except from his master's daughter, he asked for her hand in marriage, and she consented to become his wife.

This most distinguished family of Fitzwaryn are to be seen in the beautiful parish church of St Peter and St Paul in Wantage, Oxfordshire, built by one of the family in the thirteenth century. On the north side of the chancel is the dilapidated but still splendid alabaster tomb of Sir William Fitzwaryn created the twenty-sixth Garter Knight in 1361. He lies, an impressive figure in the robes of the order, beside his wife Amicia.

On a wall not far away in the main body of the church is one of the finest monumental brasses to be found in England. He is Sir Ivo Fitzwarin, the son of Sir William and his wife Amicia. He is in complete armour, his feet encased in their sollerets with rowel spurs, his sword on his left side. He wears a moustache which was fashionable during a short period of history in brass engravings, and enables one to date it to the fourteenth century. His crest was a swan between ostrich feathers.

Extinct the family certainly is but their association with one of the most beautiful legends in our history is and will surely remain immortal.

THE GRIFFITH-BOYNTONS

'OWD NANCE'

One of the strangest and most remarkable legends is that of 'Owd Nance' of Burton Agnes Hall, between Bridlington and Driffield in Humberside. This lovely red-brick mansion was begun in the reign of Queen Elizabeth and completed in the reign of James I by the architect Robert Smithson, who also built Hardwick Hall in Derbyshire. Burton Agnes is open to the public and has attracted countless thousands of visitors of whom a great many have gone expressly hoping to see the legendary skull that has caused so much interest throughout the centuries.

Next to the mansion is a most attractive Norman manor-house, encased during the seventeenth and eighteenth centuries in similar red brick to match the hall, and also open to the public. It was built by Roger de Somerville in 1175, a Staffordshire man, whose daughter Agnes probably gave the additional name to the Hall. His sister Alice married Roger de Morlay who founded a chantry in the parish church and was buried there, where are also some splendid tombs of the de Somervilles, Griffith and Boynton. In the reign of Edward I, Roger's daughter Joan married Rhys ap Griffith of Wales whose grandson came to live in the manor-house. His great-great-grandson Sir Henry Griffith began to build the Hall in 1599 to accommodate his growing family and staff. Upon his death in 1620 his three daughters, as co-heiresses, inherited a vast fortune.

All three worked hard on the building, but none more so than Anne, the youngest, whose passion for the hall was boundless. Her dedication to it became an inspiration to her sisters. Frances, the eldest sister, married Sir Matthew Boynton who later inherited Burton Agnes Hall owned to this day by the Boynton family. All was peace and harmony in the hall as the work progressed; ceasing suddenly when Anne was brutally murdered.

After her father's death Anne decided one day to pay a visit to her friends, the St Quentins, who lived at nearby Harpham Hall, another fine house. When she told her sisters they both strongly urged her not to go alone but to take the dog because of the danger of footpads. These were known in Yorkshire as the 'Wild Rangers', whose ancestors had been fed and housed in the abbeys and monasteries before their dissolution by Henry VIII. They had then nowhere to go and had turned to attacking and robbing strangers travelling about the lonely countryside and moors.

To pacify her sisters Anne took the dog and set off to see her friends. After some time she suddenly saw two men lying in the grass who sprang to their feet and came menacingly towards her. In spite of the dog's frantic barking they grabbed hold of her and demanded the diamond ring on her finger which had been a cherished gift from her mother. She refused and one man held her from behind threatening to club her down if she did not give them the ring. In the ensuing struggle the man with the club struck her unconscious to the ground. The frightened men took to their heels as the yelping dog ran after them. Only a short time later some villagers, alarmed by the frantic barking of the dog found her body. She was able to murmur that she had been going to visit Lady St Quentin and one of the villagers rushed off to tell her. Later Anne was carried to Harpham Hall to be put straight to bed and a messenger was sent at once for a doctor and a surgeon.

The next morning, though still suffering from shock and pain, she insisted upon returning to her beloved hall, only to die the following week. Before her death she sent for her sisters to make one of the strangest demands any human being could. It was to become a perpetual problem for any future owner of Burton Agnes Hall who wanted to disobey Anne's last wish. She told them that she would never sleep peacefully in her grave unless she, or part of her at least, remained in her beloved home as long as it lasted. Anne asked her sisters to give her a solemn promise that her head should be severed from her body before burial and brought within the walls of their home. She added that if they disregarded her final wish her spirit would cause nothing but disaster.

The sisters, at first indignant and then horrified, tried desperately hard to make her alter her mind but Anne was adamant. In spite of everything, they kept their silence and had the normal burial carried out, believing as they did that such a request could only have come from a badly deranged mind. Less than a week later Anne's spirit returned to the hall, just as she said it would if the vow were broken. The whole household was awakened in the dead of night by slamming doors, bells ringing and unearthly groans that terrified all to such a degree that sisters and servants spent the night together downstairs.

The weeks and months passed with alternating times of peace and appalling disturbances, and finally all the servants had been driven away. The sisters then consulted the local vicar who was horrified when they told him about the last wishes of their sister which they had disobeyed. He immediately refused to do anything, but the noises in the house grew worse to such an extent that he eventually agreed to an exhumation, though much against his will and conscience. As almost two years had passed and Burton Agnes Hall was uninhabitable, already a legend throughout the county and beyond, he finally yielded and ordered her coffin to be opened. It lay under the pavement of his church.

The body was quite uncorrupted, with no marks of decay at all, but quite mysteriously the head had severed itself from the body and become a skull. It took only seconds for the vicar to order the sisters to take the skull to the house as she had wished and to close the coffin again. This was done and it must have been a real punishment for the sister who carried the skull back into the house and placed it on a table in the great hall, one of Anne's favourite rooms.

In the last year of Anne's life, the painter Mark Gheeraerts had been commissioned to paint portraits of the three sisters together. It is still one of the most treasured pictures in Burton Agnes Hall. The three quaint figures are in their huge ruffs, their hands all identically spread upon the farthingales worn by women at that time. What is remarkable is that on the extreme right of the picture is Anne, but all in black as if the painter had been prophetic. Her small, glittering and penetrating black eyes seem to dominate the painting. Legend has it that some people have been visibly terrified by those accusing eyes.

As late as World War II the case of 'Owd Nance' was taken very seriously, if in a somewhat bizarre manner, by an American magazine which decided to investigate whether bombs had any effect upon haunted buildings and the ghosts inhabiting them. They sent a reporter to one or two famous haunted houses, the first of which was Burton Agnes Hall. The investigator was to find out if a bomb 'laid' a ghost more effectively than the customary necessity of conducting an exorcism by nine priests. The fact that Burton Agnes Hall had not been bombed did not seem to matter and the reply to him by the housekeeper who met him, the owners being away, was abrupt in the northern manner.

'Oh yes. But "Owd Nance" is still all right. Even an atom bomb wouldn't shift "Owd Nance". You come and look at her'. She then asked him to enter the hall and took him to where the picture was. The investigator stood for a long time studying the picture. 'I bet you she'll stare you out all right', said the housekeeper. 'The last time I looked at her it seemed to me she was trying to send me away. It was as much as I could do to keep from shuffling away.' It has not been recorded if the magazine continued with its investigation.

For nearly two years all was at peace in Burton Agnes Hall until one day one of the Boynton family decided to get rid of the skull and had it taken out into the garden and buried. Within hours, cries and wailings were heard all over the house, as well as constant knocking on doors as of someone trying to get in. The skull was ordered to be dug up and replaced on the table. Once more peace came. Some months later a maid who had taken a great dislike to the skull angrily threw it out of the window where a manure cart, drawn by two horses, was standing. Driver and horse became petrified as the skull fell on the cart. They remained immovable until the frantic maid ran out to explain what she had done, and the cart at once moved again, whipped on by a scared driver.

Local legends and traditions are positive that her ghost has been seen and heard by various people, particularly by Mrs Wickham-Boynton in a letter she wrote to Lord Halifax who later published it in his famous *Lord Halifax's Ghost Book*. She wrote that one day when seated in the great hall she had distinctly seen a small thin figure in a fawn dress coming through the garden and up the steps leading to the front door. She asked her husband to invite whoever it was to come in. He went but returned to say there was no one there. She was later sure, after studying the portraits that it was Anne Griffith she had seen.

Somewhere in the hall, however, Anne sleeps peacefully at last. This is because at some period of time, the skull wsa safely hidden in a niche in the wall 'somewhere in the house'. The labourer who was ordered to 'envelop' it in a wall in the house was sworn to secrecy never to divulge it. It is, however, said to be still in the great hall.

The legend of 'Owd Nance' is as much believed today as it ever was. It first originated in 1620 when Anne made her sisters vow they would always keep her in the house she loved so passionately, and they broke their promise. In a curious way Anne created her own posterity by her decision to be a part of the house she had done so much to create. There have been a great number of hauntings by skulls, many of them recorded in my previous books. Anne's was never at any time a 'Screaming Skull', as classified by a recent writer. It was rather a very determined skull that mysteriously severed itself from the body and used persistent knocking on doors to request its rightful entry to bring peace to everyone concerned. Though it may not now be seen by the public it is very decidedly present in Burton Agnes Hall, for wisely no one is going to risk disturbing it any more.

THE KILLIGREWS

THE PIRATES

If one could pick out a family with more legends than the Killigrews of Cornwall it would be a difficult task. From the moment this ancient family, who had served both kings and queens for six centuries with high honour, took to smuggling and piracy, legends abounded of their exploits. From these two pastimes they gained and lost considerable fortunes. Many of them were renowned for their ferocious tempers, courage and violence. Their origin is obscure, but the family historian claims that they were descended from a bastard male child of Richard, Earl of Cornwall, King of the Romans and brother of Henry III, by his concubine Jane de Valletorte. Their line became extinct in the male succession in 1687 when George Killigrew, son of Sir Peter, the 2nd Baronet, was killed in a drunken tavern brawl. The line continued through Anne, the younger sister of George, who married Martin Lister, the family historian. He took the name and arms of Killigrew, now extant in the present Earldom of Kimberley.

The Killigrews were captains of Henry VIII's great fortress Pendennis Castle. They were diplomats who became involved in the quarrel between Mary Queen of

Scots and Elizabeth I. Many were buried in Westminster Abbey. In 1663 they built the celebrated Theatre Royal in Drury Lane, London, burnt down in 1672 and rebuilt two years later. Charles Killigrew himself acted in his own play. They also founded the great port of Falmouth and built the Lizard lighthouse, perhaps more to further their own ends than for service to the public.

The whole of their future power and wealth began in 1383 when Simon Killigrew married Jane, daughter and heiress of the Lord of Arwenack, whose vast rich lands lay between the Helford river and the Pendennis peninsula. Here the family settled, profiting by the fast-growing trade of Penryn as a seaport. Then Henry VIII decided to build the massive Pendennis Castle on the Killigrew lands and to appoint John Killigrew as first captain of the castle. He it was who conceived the idea of entering piracy, then prevalent, as a means of increasing his already considerable wealth.

The Killigrews may justly be said to be the first great magnates of piracy. It was all thought out as a business, not as individual pirates, they were too clever for that. All robberies at sea were carefully worked out since they chose their own pirates. They paid the crews, handled all the many bribes to customs officers and appointed their own receivers of all the plunder. They took one-fifth of the actual plunder obtained not only from Cornwall but also from Devon, Dorset and south Wales. They had connections in Ireland and close links with other leading Cornish families in the same business, the Godolphins and the Bassetts, as well as the gentry. The family's position as pirates was strengthened by their appointments as captains of Pendennis Castle and chairmen of the Commissioners for Piracy in Cornwall.

Like so many of his ancestors and descendants, John Killigrew, the first captain of Pendennis Castle, was a man with a violent and uncontrollable temper, greedy and ruthless. He broke all established rules whenever he chose, raided the property of his neighbours, destroyed their crops and stole their horses and cattle. Even at the age of seventy he was a formidable figure, threatening a Privy Councillor messenger who had called at Arwenack Manor to demand the return of six rubies his son had stolen. Such was his ferocious outburst of temper that the terrified messenger fled from the house.

John Killigrew set out to rebuild Arwenack Manor which he intended to be the richest house in Cornwall. It had a great banqueting-hall and one room with a large bow-window overlooking Falmouth harbour. The house was surrounded by walls, gardens and extensive parklands. Its most important feature was the cleverly calculated secret passage that ran down into the harbour. It was to be the focal point of his entry into piracy, not as an actual pirate but as an 'aider'; more especially when Margaret, his daughter by his marriage to Elizabeth Trewinnard, married into the Godolphin family who were deeply interested in piracy, and also owned the richest tin-mines in Cornwall. John and his wife were buried in St Budock church in 1567 where there is a splendid monumental brass.

During the reign of Queen Elizabeth piracy was rampant, often helped by the queen's personal interest in obtaining wealth, however it reached her. Piracy was fully supported by the powerful squires who acted as receivers. In many cases, they were also magistrates who rarely punished suspected pirates, so long as sufficient brandy reached their cellars. Even customs officers were not amiss to a bribe. Gentry with small coves would rent them out to smugglers and pirates who found it easier landing their kegs of fine brandy there. The Killigrews, Godolphins and the Bassetts worked together very profitably.

Falmouth was probably even more important than Plymouth for pirates, and Arwenack House in its secluded part of the harbour close to Pendennis Castle naturally became the headquarters of the Killigrews as well as the residence of the chairman of the Commissioners of Piracy for Cornwall – Sir John Killigrew. Sir John was the second of four successive Johns; both his brothers Peter and Thomas were pirates. His wife Lady Mary Killigrew, the daughter of Philip Wolverstone, a gentleman pirate of Suffolk, was also involved in piracy. She had acted as his assistant in all piratical matters and became a valuable helpmate to her husband. The blood of piracy flowed in the veins of all the Killigrews. It was inevitable that, as their ill-gotten gains and riches increased, their activities would one day reach a catastrophic end. That day nearly came in 1582.

It was early evening on New Year's Day, and Lady Killigrew was sitting by the bow window of Arwenack House when her watchful eyes were suddenly alerted to something strange in the harbour. Earlier there had been a very violent storm which had forced a Spanish vessel to seek shelter. Her ladyship noticed that it was a foreign ship and at once began to make full enquiries, using the secret passage to help her. She discovered it was a Hansa ship of 140 tons burden which had dropped anchor directly in front of Arwenack House. Her two owners Philip de Orozo and Juan de Charis had walked to Penryn to spend the night in an inn. Nothing could have pleased her ladyship more. From that day she passed into Cornish local legend as the Cornish Messalina, or the Cornish Jezebel.

At midnight Lady Killigrew pushed off from shore in a boat with a few armed retainers and steering it herself she drew up alongside the Hansa ship. At the head of her armed retainers she scrambled aboard. In silence they slaughtered the unsuspecting crew and flung the bodies overboard before beginning a search of the contents. Laden with plunder, she and two of her retainers, Kendall and Hawkins, returned to Arwenack House; the others were ordered to take the ship to Ireland to dispose of the rest of the cargo. Her own loot consisted of several bolts of valuable Holland cloth and two large barrels of pieces of eight, a small fortune from one haul.

Lady Killigrew had made a fundamental and disastrous mistake. For the first time in the family's piratical history, a member had boarded a ship as a pirate and by so doing had broken their code. In the morning when the owners returned and were unable even to find their ship, they at once lodged their protest with the Commissioners for Piracy in Cornwall established in Arwenack House. Whether Sir John, the chairman, was there or not, or whether he knew what was going on, is a mystery unsolved by all who have written about the Killigrews. The verdict of the commissioners given to the unfortunate owners of the ship was that since there was no evidence to implicate any known person the jury had returned an open verdict. The ship had certainly been stolen but by whom it was impossible to say.

The Spanish owners were persistent and went to London to lay their complaint before the highest authority, the Privy Council, who instructed Sir Richard Grenville (himself not above piracy) and Edmund Tremayne to make the fullest investigation into the matter. After some considerable time and a thorough enquiry they issued orders for Lady Killigrew, Kendall and Hawkins to be sent for trial at Launceston Assizes where they were found guilty and sentenced to death. The two men were executed but Lady Killigrew was reprieved at the very last moment. When Lady Killigrew's servants were at the gallows to watch the execution 'they lamented nothing more than that they had not the company of "that old Jezebel Killigrew" at that place and begged Almighty God that some remarkable judgment might befall her and her posterity, and all those who were instrumental in promoting her pardon'. Her husband died two years later and was buried in St Budock church where his father and mother had been buried. No record exists of the fate of the

'Cornish Messalina', but the Killigrew empire continued to expand.

Fresh legends concerning the family developed up to and including the the year 1619 when the fourth John engineered and built the Lizard Lighthouse, always considered as the first English lighthouse. He did this not out of charity for the safety of ships at sea, but in order that those using the light would contribute towards it. It brought a storm of abuse and anger from the powerful Bassett family, hitherto a part of the Killigrew empire.

It had always been a local custom to use false lights from the shore to lure ships in order to plunder them. They were known as the property of the lord of the manor and brought great riches to him. The loot obtained came to be known as 'God's Grace', so that when Killigrew built the lighthouse the powerful Bassett family who were more interested in wrecking than actual piracy, though they supposedly worked together, considered 'God's Grace' had been taken away from them without their agreement or consideration. They did not know that Sir John, by characteristically underhand methods, bribes and placing pressure on important people, had obtained authority to claim a fixed contribution from passing ships guided by the lighthouse to safety from wreckers. The light went on for ten years until Trinity House took action. The present Lizard Lighthouse, open to visitors at certain times was erected in 1751, coal fires continuing to supply power until 1812.

Sir John married Jane Fermor but after eleven years divorced her because of accusations of her debauchery with Sir Nicholas Parker who had been appointed as captain of Pendennis Castle. She therefore left Arwenack House and took up lodgings in St Thomas Street, Penryn. On her death she left to Penryn Council a most curious gift of a massive silver loving cup inscribed with the words:

> From Maior to Maior to the towne of Penryn when they received mee that was in great misery. Jane Killygrew 1633.

It is their most treasured possession and the cup is held by each successive Mayor in an annual ceremony. It is difficult to understand, however, why it was ever received by Penryn in the first place, knowing as they did the reason for her divorce. It would be even more interesting to know if it was ever a part of Killigrew plunder. Winston Graham in his splendid novel about the Killigrews, *The Grove of Eagles* says in his *Postscript for Purists,* that the mystery of a substantial dowry Jane brought 'has never been cleared up, but the one reasonably well-grounded account is that the whole dowry came with her on her wedding day and was buried secretly by her two servants at Gyllyngvase – in the Arwenack grounds …' There is no record of it ever being found.

The last Sir John died heavily in debt so the Killigrew pirate empire collapsed, though the two cadet lines continued to be prosperous and thrived.

THE KIRKPATRICKS

THE WHITE SWANS

One of the saddest legends recorded in the history of any family is that of the White Swans of Closeburn Castle, the home for seven centuries of the distinguished Scottish family of Kirkpatrick. Within the castle grounds was a small lake to which every year a pair of swans would come, bringing joy to the family when they heard and saw them, until the day when tragedy struck both family and birds. All that remains today of the thirteenth-century castle is the square tower house clearly seen from the village of Closeburn on the A76 from Dumfries to Kilmarnock.

The family name was derived from Kirk, the Scottish name for 'church', and Patrick from the saint of that name to whom a chapel, formerly in the grounds, was dedicated. They have a most impressive defiant crest and motto on their coat of arms, originating with Sir Roger Kirkpatrick, one of the first who stood up for Robert the Bruce. According to *Burke's Peerage,* 'on returning from striking John Cummin in the church at Dumfries, Sir Roger went into the church exclaiming "I'll make sicker (sure)" and then gave several stabs with his dagger.' Thus their crest is a hand holding a dagger distilling blood, and their motto 'I make sure'.

Their lineage began with Ivone Kirkpatrick during the reign of David I of Scotland (1123–53) who was witness to the Charter of Robert Bruce the elder, granting fishing rights to the monks of Abbeyholm. His grandson, Sir Roger, married Euphemia, a daughter of Robert the Bruce, and received from Alexander II (1214–19) a confirmatory charter of the lands of Closeburn. The whole family entered into years of struggle and warfare when Edward I invaded Scotland and captured the castle of Caerlaverock in 1300. Though his tomb in Westminster Abbey bears the words 'Here lies Edward the Hammer of the Scots', he never succeeded in forcing them into his dream of an undivided England. He waged war ceaselessly until his death, first against William Wallace, then against Robert the Bruce who defeated the king's son, the worthless Edward II, in the battle of Bannockburn in 1314.

A second Sir Roger Kirkpatrick captured the important castles of Durisdeer and Caerlaverock in 1355 but was murdered two years later in the latter Castle. His son Ivone had confirmation of Closeburn in 1409. Throughout their long history each successive heir seems to have added honours to the family name.

Through all these years and events the Kirkpatrick legend of the White Swans was handed down from each head of the family to the heir.

The first visit of the birds came far back in their history at a time when the wife of the lord was dangerously ill. It was because her life was saved by a miracle that the family were certain that the arrival of the swans had caused it.

Thus from that time the swans were regarded as the harbingers of joy. They became even more convinced when one of the heirs to the lordship was on the point of death. Their joy was great when they heard the heavy wingbeats above the castle, before seeing the swans swooping down to the lake, crossing it, then gliding towards the anxiously watching family. That same night the heir recovered. It therefore became of vital importance that each heir should be made aware of the tradition.

One day, however, tragedy struck the family, so that from that moment the beautiful white birds came no longer as harbingers of joy but as warnings of impending death for one of the family. Robert, a thirteen-year-old son was in Edinburgh on a holiday and during that time had been taken to the theatre for a performance of *The Merchant of Venice*. In a speech given by Portia to her lover Bassanio deciding which to choose of the three caskets containing a message from her she says:

> Let musick sound while he doth make his choice,
> Then if he lose, he makes a swan-like end,
> Fading in musick …

It is doubtful if, at the age of thirteen, Robert fully grasped the meaning of Shakespeare's lines, but the mention of swans, so firmly planted in his mind and the possibility that they had death-songs struck him as one it would be interesting to put to the test when he returned home. He was a good hunter and a fine archer for his age and the very next morning he went down early to the lake. There gliding gracefully and trustingly towards him, seeking bread perhaps, came one of the swans. In a swift move Robert shot his arrow which buried itself in the swan's breast. He waited expectantly for the death-song but none came as the bird began to sink in the blood-stained water.

Robert, horrified at what he saw and terrified at what would happen to him, waded swiftly into the water to lift the bird from the lake to hide it somewhere before any of the family discovered what he had done. He frantically dug at the marshy and sodden edge of the lake until he had made a shallow place to hide the bird until he was able to fetch a spade and later dig a deeper hole. There was no sign of the other swan, nor the day after, nor at all, and the family supposed they had departed together and would return a year later, but they did not.

Several years passed before one spring, quite early in the morning, the heavy wing-beat of a swan was heard above the house and all the family rushed out to the lake to see the beautiful bird glide down to the water and move with elegance and dignity towards them. Robert, unable to conceal his terror, saw its breast glowing red as it had when he had first shot his arrow into it. The family, so happy and excited, believing it brought good tidings for the master who was ill, did not even notice Robert's terror as he moved away from them and back to the castle. The swan remained there for a week before the family heard the heavy wing-beats they knew so well, watching anxiously as the bird departed. The master died that night. No longer was the bird a harbinger of joy but one of ill-omen and therefore to be feared. Years passed before the swan reappeared, its visit followed shortly by news of one of the family drowned in a shipwreck.

The year 1685 was a momentous one for Sir Thomas Kirkpatrick. He was created a Baronet of Nova Scotia 'for fidelity to Charles the First'. He had also built the mansion of Closeburn with stone from the castle, and was celebrating his third marriage. A great wedding breakfast was being held after which Roger, son of the second marriage, made his customary walk down to the lake when he saw with horror the swan of ill-omen gliding towards him, its breast glowing red. Unable to continue watching he turned back and ran towards the house where his father, seeing his white face, asked what was the matter. He told him that he had seen the swan, but his father only laughed it off and went back to the party. That night, quite unexpectedly, Roger died. All in the house heard the wing-beats of the departing swan, which nevermore returned.

The final blow came to the family on the night of 29 August 1718 when Closeburn mansion was razed to the ground by a fire caused by drunken servants which destroyed all the private papers, documents, portraits and furniture. In spite of this disaster, this most distinguished family is still extant after seven centuries, justifying its most remarkable legend and their proud motto: 'I make sure'.

THE LLEWELLYNS

THE DEATH OF GELERT

One of the most famous and well known Welsh legends is that concerned with the Gwynedd village of Beddgelert and Llewellyn the Great. It is said to have been founded on a foreign story mentioned in the celebrated Red Book of Hergest (*Llyr Coch Hergest*), 1373–1425, preserved in the library of Jesus College, Oxford. It has been stated that the legend probably originated in the *Arabian Nights* and is one of an amalgam of myths and legends from the folklore of Arabia, Persia, India, England, Ireland and Wales. So many legends have come down to us, first orally, by wandering story-tellers in return for hospitality given to them in the houses of the nobility; in the fifteenth century they were recorded in manuscript and later printed.

The legend of Llewellyn the Great and the hound he named Gelert, dates from the early twelfth century. It would be interesting to know whether the dog's name came from the village or the village was named after the dog. The legend begins and ends with stark and dramatic brevity. Llewellyn was a great hunter and his hound always accompanied him wherever he went, especially the chase. One day, however, he was completely puzzled by the dog's stubborn refusal to go out with him, in spite of all his master's pleadings and commands, and Llewellyn eventually went hunting without him.

When he returned later in the day he was met by a jubilant and happy dog, bouncing up and down to greet his master. Suddenly Llewellyn was appalled to see blood upon the dog's mouth and paws. Swiftly noticing that the cradle where his baby had been was empty, in blind fury he drew his sword, drove it into the dog's body and killed it. As he passed into the next room he saw the baby safe and well on the floor, but surrounded by morsels of bleeding flesh, more blood, and the mangled head of a wolf. It was only then that the horror of what he had done overcame him as he realized that he had murdered his beloved dog who had remained at home to guard the baby and had killed the wolf. In remorse and sorrow, Llewellyn had a special tomb made in which Gelert's dead body was placed, and it is said to have been buried under a mound known as Gelert's Grave in what is now Snowdonia National Park. The mound has been visited by thousands of visitors, especially dog-lovers, who have read or heard of the sad legend. The fact that it has now been judged to be a natural mound of the Commission of Ancient and Historical Monuments in no way affects the faithful pilgrimages made by countless lovers of legend.

Another less-known legend concerning Llewellyn the Great belongs to nearby Anglesey (known in the *Mabinogion* as *The Island of the Mighty*). It relates particularly to Aberffraw and its parish church of St Mary and St Nicholas where, in the south porch, lies a stone coffin traditionally said to have been that of Princess Joan, illegitimate daughter of the English King John, and second wife of Llewellyn the Great.

The church was built in the fourteenth century for the use of the English garrison, probably while Beaumaris Castle was being built for Edward I, a massive structure never completed for lack of money. Whether the garrison had thrown out the coffin is conjectural, but it was being used as a horse trough when it was discovered and restored to the church. This stone coffin is a complete mystery, for Princess Joan died in 1237, a century before the church was built. It is inconceivable that such a great ruler as Llewellyn the Great would not have had a splendid funeral and the coffin placed in a church. Where was it before Aberffraw church was built? Was it discovered for the first time when the church was being built and then thrown out? If so, what happened to the body? How did the coffin become a horse trough? Like so many traditions and legends the story of Joan's coffin remains an insoluble mystery.

Llewellyn the Great was born in 1194, died 1240, and was twice married, first to a Welsh woman, then to Princess Joan. His grandson was Llewellyn the Last who died 1282. During their lifetime both are said to have held court in the palace of Aberffraw, though there is no evidence that such a palace existed. The Welsh Herald of Arms Extraordinary in *Royal and Princely Heraldry in Wales* states the following facts: 'After centuries of strife Llewellyn the Great succeeded in uniting Wales, and was recognized as Prince of Wales by King Henry III. Llewellyn's grandson, Llewellyn ap Gruffydd, was also so recognized, but he fell foul of King Edward I and was defeated in 1282'.

Edward I created the first English Prince of Wales in 1301. Edward III created his son, the Black Prince, the second English Prince of Wales and the title has descended down to the present day.

THE LUCYS AND THE SHAKESPEARES

WILLIAM SHAKESPEARE

One of the most notable legends is that of de Lucy of Charlecote and Shakespeare, which originated in Charlecote Park, Warwickshire – the beautiful home of the Lucy family presented by them to the National Trust and open to the public. By accepted local and family tradition, England's most famous poet and playwright was caught poaching, brought before Sir Thomas Lucy, severely punished and might well have lost his life. Instead he used his great talents to have his revenge on Sir Thomas, strangely leading to a final reconciliation with the family.

In the year 1189 Sir Walter de Charlecote inherited Charlecote from his father Thurstane. Sir Walter's grandson, Sir William de Lucy inherited the property in 1247. According to the heraldist Sir William Dugdale he adopted this name because, it is surmised, his wife came of the ancient and illustrious family of de Lucy, Lords of Cockermouth in Cumbria. He was certainly the first Lucy of Charlecote, direct ancestor of Edmund Lucy and Sir Thomas Lucy, who in 1551 inherited and rebuilt Charlecote Park. He was a Knight of the Shire and important enough to entertain Queen Elizabeth at Charlecote Park in August 1572. Thirteen years later, as magistrate in 1585, he unwittingly became known throughout the world in an infamous legend.

The history of the Shakespeare family is a far more confusing one. It is an astonishing fact that the story of one of the greatest playwrights and poets should present so many problems in research, and it is entirely due to the invaluable parish registers that we know anything at all. According to L.G. Pine's essay in *Burke's Peerage*, it is because of the parish registers that we are able to trace the family through the Harts, the descendants of William's sister Joan, from 1552 to 1952. More revealing is the fact that Mary Arden, Shakespeare's mother, was one of only three families with pedigrees traceable in the male line from pre-Conquest times.

John Shakespeare, the poet's father, was styled in 1556 as a glover and since he could not write he made his mark on all documents by a pair of dividers used by glovers. He traded in barley, timber and wool and was considered to be a man of substance, a yeoman under the degree of gentleman. His marriage to Mary Arden, his landlord's daughter increased his prosperity, enabling him to buy and sell properties and houses and eventually to apply for and be granted a coat of arms. He did this at the instigation of his son William, 'To show the world I am a gentleman', which as heir he considered himself to be. One might well wonder why the poet's father was prepared to go to the considerable expense of a coat of arms, except that by Elizabethan times coat armour had become the mark of a gentleman. The Shakespeare arms were: Gold, on a black bend a gold tilting-spear, point upwards; for his crest a falcon with wings displayed standing on a wreath supporting a spear, headed and steeled silver, fixed on a helmet with mantles and tassels with the motto 'Nons sans droit'. There are two interesting points about John Shakespeare's granted arms. The spear was obviously a pun on his own name, and the falcon might have been a reference to the Falcon Inn in Bidford which he frequented as later did his son. Local legend has it that William once joined a drinking party there and became so drunk that he collapsed on the Stratford road under a crab-apple tree, thereafter known as Shakespeare's Crab-tree even as late as 1824, when it was felled.

The main legend linking the two families of Shakespeare and Lucy is a proud tradition of the Lucy family, in spite of the revenge taken by the poet for the punishment meted out to him by Sir Thomas Lucy for poaching rabbits and stealing six venison in his own park. Such is their pride at being linked to the greatest poet and dramatist in England that in the great hall of Charlecote Park there is a quarter-length bust of Shakespeare. According to Richard Davies, 'William Shakespeare, born in Stratford-upon-Avon in Warwickshire about 1563, was much given to all unluckiness in stealing venison and rabbits, particularly from Sir Lucy who had him oft whip't and sometimes imprisoned.' The punishment was meted out to the poet in the great hall of Charlecote Park where Sir Thomas, as local magistrate, presided. The whipping might well have been flogging for in those times punishment was severe for stealing, most especially venison, which, and again from the words of Richard Davies, this 'at last made him fly his country'.

There are naturally various versions of this great legend, but like many young people throughout the centuries, Shakespeare set out for London, where he became first an actor of plays and then a great dramatist.

As a parting gift to Sir Thomas, Shakespeare wrote a ribald ballad about him and stuck or nailed it on the entrance gate to Charlecote Park. The actual ballad was lost for a time, but just before his death in 1703, Oldys, the Norroy King of Arms, and a great scholar, left this ballad with other valuable material for a *Life of Shakespeare*. The source Oldys gave was in his own words:

> There was a very aged gentleman living in the neighbourhood of Stratford (where he died fifty years hence) who had not only heard from several old people in that town, of Shakespeare's transgression but could remember the first stanza of the bitter ballad which, repeating to one acquaintance, he preserved it in writing and here it is, neither better nor worse, but faithfully transcribed from the copy, which his relation very contentedly communicated to me.
>
> A parliament member, a justice of peace,
> At home a poor scare-crow, at London an asse,
> If lowsy is Lucy, as some volke miscalle it,
> Then Lucy is lowsie, whatever befall it;
> He thinke himself greate
> Yet an asse in his state
> We allowe by his eares, but with asses to mate.
> If Lucy is lowsie, as some volke miscalle it,
> Sing lowsie Lucy, whatever befalle it.

An even more malicious and scurrilous ballad

supposedly also written by Shakespeare was discovered by a Cambridge Professor of Greek in 1690 who had heard it from an old woman.

Sir Thomas was too covetous
To covet so much deer,
When horns enough upon his head
Most plainly did appear.

Had not his worship one deer left,
What then he had a wife
Took pains enough to find him horns
Shou'd hold him during life.

It is in two of his plays, *Henry IV* and *The Merry Wives of Windsor* that Shakespeare continued his attacks on Sir Thomas, caricaturing him as Justice Shallow with mocking words about the Lucy coat of arms (a red shield three silver luces heads pointing upwards as if for air). A luce was a fish, known as a pike or Jack. Again and again the real Sir Thomas Lucy would remind people that his coat of arms was 'an old coat. A very old coat indeed.' This fussy, pompous, irritating Justice of the Peace and magistrate, 'Coram', 'Castelorum', 'Gentleman born' and 'Armigero' was pilloried by Shakespeare.

The poet's reference to his own poaching emerges when Justice Shallow meets Falstaff, who borrowed one thousand pounds from him and never paid it back. 'You have beaten my men, killed my deer, and broken open my lodge.' 'But not kissed your keeper's daughter', answers the fat knight. 'The dozen white louses do become an old coat well,' says Sir Hugh Evans to Justice Shallow, 'it is a familiar beast', he adds, referring to a louse and not a luce.

According to Richard Davies, who died in 1708, probably the most authentic authority, the first to record the deer-stealing by the poet and the first to disclose his religion, says: 'Shakespeare dyed April 23, 1616, probably at Stratford, for there he is buryd, and hath a Monument on which he laid a heavy curse upon anyone who shall remove his bones. He dyed a Papist'.

In the Lucy Chapel in Charlecote church are the three fine tombs of the first three Sir Thomas Lucys. The second one had fourteen children by his second wife, formerly Constance Kingsmill of Highclere in Hampshire, a great heiress. She is seen kneeling beside his tomb, heavily dressed in widow's weeds, a quite remarkable figure.

It was the third Sir Thomas who healed the deep wound given to his grandfather by William Shakespeare when he pilloried him in revenge for his punishment. The first object one sees upon entering the impressive Great Hall at Charlecote is a quarter-length shining white marble bust of the poet, balanced on the other side of the fireplace by the quarter-length shining white marble bust of Sir Thomas himself. It would have been a perfect ending to a perfect legend had the two been finally reconciled and dined together in the splendid dining-room. It was a generous gesture indeed by the grandson of 'Justice Shallow' to have them put there together in the very room where the flogging took place.

THE MACLEODS

THE FAIRY FLAG

There can be few more beautiful settings for a castle than Dunvegan Castle on the Isle of Skye, stronghold and home of the chiefs of the Clan MacLeod for seven centuries. It stands impressively above Loch Dunvegan, its seagate, gun court and curtain wall which Leod built in 1270 still visible. What is so wonderful about it all is the fact that though it is still lived in as a family home, it is open to the public and welcomes tens of thousands of visitors and members of the clan from all over the world.

When a family has lived in one place for so long, it naturally accumulates treasures of which it is justifiably proud. The MacLeods have a great number of such treasures, the famous Fairy Flag, the Dunvegan Cup, Rory Mor's Horn, the Dunvegan Armorial, and Sir Walter Scott's manuscripts and letters from many distinguished people. These have all been preserved throughout the centuries of constant wars between the clans, notably with the MacDonalds, Lords of the Isles and Earls of Ross; through it all the MacLeods survived and kept their castle, proudly reflected in the simple words of the motto above the crest of their coat of arms 'Hold fast'.

Their most precious possession is the Fairy Flag, its very existence based on a legend, unique in folklore but implicitly accepted and believed in by every member of this ancient clan. This tattered and torn seventh-century silk flag is more probably a banner since it was carried in two wars by the MacLeods, and is believed to have come from the island of Rhodes.

There have been many stories and legends about the Fairy Flag, but the MacLeods firmly believe their own tradition. Iain, the fourth clan chief who had lived for twenty years with his fairy wife, so they say, one day decided he must return to his former life and declared he must leave her. They parted on Fairy Bridge, some miles from the castle and as a parting gift she gave him the Fairy Flag. She told him it could only be waved three times when the clan was in peril and it would bring them victory. Their first victory was in 1490 in the battle of Langdale, the second in 1580 at Trumpan. Such is the belief in its power that throughout World War II, the MacLeods serving in the RAF all carried photographs of it. One other tradition was that the Flag, when laid on the matrimonial bed, would bring a fruitful union to the chief of the clan on his marriage. It is very doubtful indeed if the darned and tattered flag was ever used for such a purpose.

The Dunvegan Lullaby is yet another legend connected with the Flag, it is still sung in parts of the Isle of Skye. In the fifteenth century when the wife of the Chief Iain Borb gave birth to their child, a fairy came to the castle, sought and found the infant-heir, took him on her knees and wrapped him in the Fairy Flag before returning him to his cradle, singing the lullaby to send him to sleep. The nurse, spellbound by what she saw, remembered the melody and words of the Dunvegan Lullaby and passed them on to other islanders. Once again, the very condition of the Flag makes one doubt whether it was ever wrapped round a child's body.

The Dunvegan Cup is another heirloom. It was given to the 15th Chief, Sir Rory Mor, by the O'Neills of Ulster in 1595 for supporting their cause against England, but the cup itself is known to be of a much earlier age, for legends associate it with a tenth-century King of Ulster, Niall Glundub; the silverwork is dated 1493. The inscription round the top is in Latin stating that it was carried out for Katherine, ancestor of the O'Neills and a descendant of King Niall.

Yet another family treasure is Rory Mor's Horn. This is the horn of a Kyloe bull, a species of Hebridean cattle. The legend is that the 3rd Chief Malcolm took on a wild bull in single combat during a visit he made to his father-in-law in the county of Argyll. The onlookers watching excitedly cried out to him, 'Hold Fast MacLeod!' and a moment later he broke the beast's neck. This feat is proudly recognized in the motto and crest of the MacLeod coat of arms. It shows a bull's head facing straight out and above it the motto 'Hold fast'. A unique ceremony takes place with this celebrated cup which holds a bottle and three-quarters of claret. Tradition requires that the contents should be drained by the heir to the chieftainship at his coming of age 'without setting down or falling down.'

The fifteenth-century dungeon still exhibits grim evidence of the lot of any prisoner of the MacLeods. There are the heavy weights and chains used both to torture and to prevent any possible chance of escape. In those days prisoners were shown little mercy and the dungeon formed an integral part of the keep. Prisoners were bundled from the gatehouse to a trap in the floor where they were shackled and lowered, or more probably thrown, into a pit sixteen feet below and left to die of cold or starvation.

Each and every room in this beautiful castle has individual taste and charm, notably the drawing-room with its Zoffany portraits and grand piano. There are other fine portraits, notably that of Dame Flora MacLeod the celebrated 28th Clan Chief. MacLeods from all over the world are bound together by the strongest of ties, and especially by the Clan Parliament formed in Dunvegan Castle by Dame Flora MacLeod, that most dearly loved of all the recent Clan Chiefs. She died in 1976 at the age of 92.

All that she herself felt as a chieftain was expressed in her own unforgettable words when she said of the clan family: '... beyond and outside divisions between nations, countries and continents ... It takes no note of age or rank or wealth, success or failure ... Clanship embraces them all.'

THE FAMILY OF KING MARK

TRISTAN AND ISEULT

The story of Tristan and Iseult has been called the greatest love-story in the world, immortalized by Richard Wagner in his great opera *Tristan und Isolde*. Like so many legends it is founded on different accounts from various twelfth-century romanticists. The earliest account seems to have been that in the lost manuscript of Thomas the Norman during the reign of Henry the Second from which Beroul, a Breton, took most of the story, as did Einhart von Oberge and later Gottfried von Strasburg, both Germans. The most authoritative account seems to have been that of the unknown Beroul who wrote some 3,000 verses, most of which have been lost. *Tristan and Iseult in Cornwall*, a little book by E.R.M. Ditmas, contains part of this translated poem and gives ample evidence of Beroul's knowledge of Cornwall. Beroul was the only one to have visited and lived in Cornwall.

In the fifth century Gorlois or Gourles reigned over Cornwall. His wife was Igraine who was seduced by Uther Pendragon with the aid of Merlin's magic and bore a son, King Arthur. Charles Henderson, the brilliant young Cornish historian suggests in his *Essays in Cornish History* that Gorlois was succeeded by Mark. Therefore it is more than likely he was the son of Gorlois and Igraine. Is it possible that King Arthur and King Mark were half-brothers? It is significant that during the trial to prove Iseult's chastity to King Mark she demanded that King Arthur also be present and pass judgment.

In the sixth century King Mark ruled over Cornwall and part of Wales. He had a sister named Blancheflor who had married Rivalan, either a Breton nobleman or a lord from Lyonesse, that mysterious kingdom between Land's End and the Scilly Isles now lost beneath the sea. Blancheflor died when giving birth to Tristan, and the care and upbringing of the infant was entrusted to Governal in Lyonesse. Twenty years later both appeared in Mark's palace of Castle Dore near Fowey in Cornwall. Tristan, whose relationship to Mark was unknown to both of them, wished to prove himself as a knight.

His opportunity was not long in coming for Mark's overlord, the king of Ireland, had sent a fearsome warrior named Morholt, the queen's brother, to demand the annual tribute. This had at first been tin, then silver and gold, but now he demanded young men and girls who would become slaves. To refuse this tribute meant a challenge to single combat, and since none of Mark's barons were brave enough Tristan offered to fight Morholt. The battle was a fierce and bloody one ending in Tristan being severely wounded, but Morholt was mortally wounded by a sword-blade that cut through his helmet deep into his skull where a piece of the blade broke off and remained embedded in the bone. The Irish embarked with their dying champion and Tristan became a hero at once, and was acknowledged to be a knight by his uncle, causing intense jealousy amongst the barons.

Not long after this Tristan had another chance to prove his powers. One day when his uncle was in the palace gardens he watched two swallows fighting over a single golden hair in the beak of one of them, the long strand of hair falling to the ground as both birds flew away. Mark picked it up and took it to Tristan saying that he would marry the woman with such beautiful golden hair wherever she lived and whoever she was. Tristan at once set off to find the woman, going first to Ireland disguised as a merchant and calling himself Tantris.

He had not been long there before he heard that a terrible dragon was devastating the countryside to such an extent that the king had offered his fair-haired daughter, the Princess Iseult, in marriage to anyone who could kill it. Tristan at once set about finding the dragon and after a bloody battle in which his horse was killed and he himself wounded, he killed the dragon and as proof cut out its tongue. After wandering for some time he collapsed from exhaustion. Meanwhile the king's steward had found the dragon and cut off its head to claim the princess's hand in marriage. Iseult, who loathed the steward and totally disbelieved his story set out to find Tristan. She, like her mother, also named Iseult, had great gifts of healing and managed to heal his wounds and give him hospitality.

One day whilst Tristan was taking a bath, Iseult amused herself by examining his armour and his sword when to her horror she found a notch in its blade which caused her to remember the splinter of steel she had found embedded in her uncle Morholt's skull when his body was brought back from Cornwall. In a fury she was about to kill Tristan, when her faithful companion Brangane held her back, reminding her that if she killed Tristan she would be forced to marry the steward whom she hated. The king then offered Iseult to Tristan as his reward; but when he heard Tristan's story of a promise of marriage by King Mark to whoever had such beautiful hair as the strand Tristan now showed him, both he and his daughter agreed she should be Queen of Cornwall and departed for that land. Before they left, the queen, Iseult's mother, handed a love-potion to Brangane to be given to King Mark on the wedding night.

They set out on the long journey to Cornwall, but unfortunately on the voyage the love-potion was shared accidentally by Tristan and Iseult, who at once fell desperately and uncontrollably in love with each other. They finally came to Castle Dore. When Mark saw the beautiful Iseult Tristan had found for him he fell deeply in love with Iseult at first sight. In fear of being found out in her infidelity Iseult persuaded Brangane to take her place in the marriage bed on the wedding night, for she was now hopelessly in love with Tristan. Brangane agreed, for she blamed herself for her carelessness over the love-potion, and the wedding passed without discovery by the king.

The barons, more suspicious than before of the Tristan they now hated, plotted to have him banished. They soon noticed that during the many absences from court King Mark was forced to make, Tristan and Iseult were never apart. What they did not know was that both lovers were now afraid their illicit love would be discovered. Iseult herself feared that Brangane would one day give her secret away and she even considered poisoning her to prevent it. Brangane, however, swore that she would never betray her and thus was saved from death.

Inevitably the jealous barons caused Mark himself to become suspicious, finally agreeing to his dwarf's suggestion that he should be witness to a conclusive trap he had set for the lovers. The king was to announce his departure but would return secretly that night to his chamber where the dwarf said he would see for himself what would happen. He had scattered flour between the beds of the king and queen so that if Tristan moved across he would leave footprints in it. Late that night they both saw Tristan leap from the king's bed to the queen's bed. Unfortunately Tristan had been wounded in a boar hunt that day and the jump caused the wound to reopen spilling drops of blood on the flour. Hearing a disturbance Tristan had only time for a hasty embrace with Iseult before he leapt back again as Mark and the dwarf, holding a lighted candle, exposed the guilty lovers.

In an outburst of fury Mark ordered them to be seized, their hands bound behind their backs, and sentenced them to death. Tristan managed to escape. Mark, when told of this, vented all his fury into merciless treatment of his queen. The next morning she was led out of the palace, her wrists bound so tightly that blood dripped down her fingers. As if Beroul were actually witnessing this, he tells us that she wore a grey-brown robe over which her plaited hair fell as far as her feet. All the people wept when they saw her and even when Dinas the seneschal knelt before Mark to plead for her the king ignored him. The execution was delayed when the leader of a band of ragged lepers suggested that Iseult would suffer far more if she were handed over to them for their enjoyment. To the horror of all the people the king agreed and she was led away by the diseased and filthy lepers. None there knew that Tristan was hiding nearby in a thicket, but as the band passed he leapt out and snatched Iseult, rushing with her into deeper hiding in Morois.

Here they hid for some months, during which time Tristan's tutor Governal found and joined them, bringing with him Tristan's armour and horse. Life was hard for them, living off what Tristan could kill, mostly venison, cutting branches to make shelters at night, the ground strewn with gathered leaves. In spite of all these hardships the power of the love-potion still obsessed them with passion and desire. In their wanderings they came upon the hermitage of Brother Ogrin. He recognized Tristan, told him there was a price on his head and urged him to repent, but both he and Iseult declared there was no possibility of their ever parting so deep was their love inspired by the power of the love-potion. Brother Ogrin, pitying them, allowed them to stay the night in his hermitage.

More months of wandering passed until one day a forester discovered the two lovers lying side by side fast asleep. He rode at once through the forest back to Castle Dore to claim the reward. The king ordered him to lead him back to the place where they still lay asleep. The king trod softly towards the lovers, drawing his sword to kill them, but was bewildered by what he saw. They lay there so peacefully and innocently, unaware of their danger, that the king became filled with pity. Between the two lay Tristan's sword. In a few moments the king changed this for his own gold-hilted one and, seeing the wedding-ring on Iseult's finger, he changed it for his own, leaving his gloves across her breast, before returning with the forester to the palace. When the lovers awoke they were terrified at what had happened. More even than their fear was their sudden realization that the love-potion had ceased, leaving them both full of guilt. It was the day following the feast of St John and after three years of wanderings the spell had broken.

Beroul himself in his poem speaks in the present tense as if he himself had been a witness, something he continued to do until the end. It is from this moment that his knowledge of Cornwall is evident for all the places he mentions are there today. In the writing of this book, the author and his wife have retraced the ancient tracks of the area, discovering the remains of Castle Dore, the Morois forest, Lancien, Blanchland, St Sampson church, Milltown, Lostwithiel and many other places accessible today. It is Beroul's love of his subject and of Cornwall that makes this beautiful legendary love-story unique to England and its great folklore heritage.

At the moment of the lovers' awakening, Beroul tells us of Tristan's sorrow and guilt of all that he had given up … his honour as a knight, the affection and trust of his uncle … He realized how Iseult must have suffered for him, and that he must now exchange their life together for the life of a ragged and dishonoured fugitive. When he returns to Iseult '… he is full of grief and repentance and he finds that she too has changed. At last they agree to seek King Mark's pardon.' To do this they went to Brother Ogrin in his hermitage to ask his pardon for what had happened, explaining that Tristan would leave the country if the king would forgive and take back Iseult his wife. Ogrin pardoned them and agreed to act as intermediary which ended in the king's expressed wish to receive back his queen at the Perilous Ford in three days time. Tristan was to leave the country.

On the appointed day Tristan accompanied Iseult to the field of reconciliation before leaving her in sorrow, for in spite of the fading of the love-potion they were still deeply in love. Iseult gave him her ring with a jasper stone, telling him that if ever he needed her he was to send this ring with a messenger as proof that it came from Tristan.

Tristan went back to the forest with Governal to make up his mind where he would go, telling Iseult she would find him there for some time if ever she needed him. Within three months, a messenger sent by Iseult found him in the forest, to tell him that the barons demanded that the king should force Iseult to face a trial by ordeal to prove her innocence. She was therefore forced to agree and had chosen Blanchland as the trial place. She begged him to meet her there in disguise as a leper to carry her across a deep stream leading to the place which he already knew.

Yet again Beroul seems to have visited the appointed place. It was known to him as a hillock above a marsh leading into Blanchland at Mal Pas, and there was Tristan 'dressed in rough garments with a wide stained cloak and broken footgear. He carried a leper's crutch, a wooden bowl and bottle, and the clapper that warns people to keep away.' Iseult arrived 'very splendid in a robe of silk from Bagdad', ordering Tristan to carry her across. He pretended not to understand. She told him he must be her ass to carry her across. Finally he helped her on to his back, his head and neck between her legs as he staggered across the deep mud supported by his crutch, where she slipped off his back leaving him to return to the forest.

The next day, before a vast crowd, the trial by ordeal began. Such trials have for centuries taken place in India and the Far East requiring a woman to prove her innocence to her bridegroom by treading across hot iron ploughshares. This, however, was not the severe trial Iseult had to pass. It took place, Beroul tells us, before both King Mark and King Arthur, by Iseult's wish since she had asked King Arthur to pass judgment and not her husband. King Arthur gave his promise that he would tell the huge crowd gathered to see the ordeal that he would severely punish any person who, should Iseult prove her innocence, accuse her afterwards.

In a great silence the Queen stepped forward to the embroidered silk cloth upon which were assembled holy relics of saints. There were gold and silver caskets, crosses and shrines from all over the land. There she swore her solemn oath by St Hilary.

> No man has come between my thighs,
> Except the leper who made himself a beast of burden
> Who carried me over the ford,
> And the King Mark my husband.

It is strange that Iseult swore by St Hilary because the Cornish church she was so familiar with was St Sampson in Golant not very far from Fowey. Tradition has it that both she and the King held their masses there, and that Iseult gave her best dress to the church to be brought out on feast days. It is even likely that she and the king were married there.

Unfortunately Beroul's long poem ended shortly after describing the ordeal, except that he relates that the two lovers met once again. Gottfried von Strasburg also died before completing his prose narrative. It is now that confusion dominates this wonderful secular love story. That Tristan left Cornwall seems to be generally accepted. Malory's version, based on another prose version says that King Mark discovered the lovers together again in the forest where he killed Tristan with a poisoned spear. Einhart von Oberge finishes his work with the death of both lovers in Brittany but with a different ending from other versions.

There is one enigmatic sequel, however, to the stories, and that is the most interesting early monument, the Tristan Stone between Fowey and the site of King Mark's palace at Castle Dore, seen by countless thousands of visitors to Cornwall over the centuries. This stone, originally erected nearby in 550 AD and inscribed 'Drustans hic iacit', which translated reads 'Here lies Tristan'. The inscription then reads on 'Cunomori filius', which means 'Son of Cunomorus'. According to F.E. Halliday, Cornish historian, Cuonomorius was Mark. He adds carefully and diplomatically that the story, '... must not be pressed too far, though it is quite possible that the original relationship was changed to give a less shocking version.'

The origins of the love-story has caused much confusion. Malory in his *Morte d'Arthur* is totally inaccurate, replacing as it does, Mark's Castle Dore by Tintagel; one must remember that he was writing a thousand years later than Beroul. That Tristan did go to Brittany is more than reasonable since the love-story claims to have been a Breton legend pure and simple. He went to fight for King Howel of Brittany against a neighbouring enemy and was rewarded for his services by being offered the king's daughter in marriage, named Iseult also, the third in this story, but called 'Iseult of the White Hands'. Though Tristan had no affection for her he married her. Her brother was Kaherdin and according to Einhart von Oberge, they went back to Cornwall together to see Iseult in order to prove Tristan's sworn statement to Kaherdin that Iseult, Queen of Cornwall was far more beautiful than 'Iseult of the White Hands'. This wholly improbable story ends with the two men quarrelling and Tristan being killed with a poisoned spear.

In another account they returned to Brittany where Tristan became wounded and, entrusting a messenger to carry the ring Iseult had given him long ago, begged her to come and cure his wound. The messenger was also instructed to tell the Queen that if she were coming a white sail was to be hoisted on the return voyage, if not, a black one. Tristan's wife, 'Iseult of the White Hands' overheard the instructions and in jealous revenge waited for the ship which came bearing a white sail. Tristan begged her to tell him whether the sail was white, but she told him it was black. Tristan died as Iseult landed, and finding her lover dead she died also. The two were buried side by side. On their grave two saplings were planted and as they grew the branches intertwined, uniting them in death as it had in life in their undying love. Einhart von Oberge, however, gave a significantly different version, ending his account as follows:

> King Mark arrived in search of his queen and heard at last of the full story of the love-potion. Full of sorrow at the loss of his beloved wife and nephew, he ordered that their bodies be returned and buried with honour in Cornwall.

It is a pity that Beroul's manuscript was lost, for it is a poem revealing a great sympathy of and love for Cornwall, where he lived and which he described with such accuracy. The story of Tristan and Iseult remains a remarkable and beautiful legend, one of the greatest love-stories in the world and, if one accepts all that Beroul has written, perhaps the most English.

Indeed, there is a particularly English aspect according to Ditmas. He writes:

> The sword with which Tristan killed the Morholt has a niche in English history. One of the swords carried in the coronation of Henry IV was called the *Curtana* and had a 'broken' point. It was almost certainly the 'Sword of Tristan', once one of King John's treasures. Later it became the symbol of the King's Mercy and a replica is still carried in the coronation procession.

THE THROCKMORTONS

THE NEWBURY COAT

For almost six centuries the Throckmorton family have occupied Coughton Court, that most beautiful Warwickshire mansion on the edge of the Forest of Arden. It is not far away from Charlecote Park, home of the ancient family of Lucy. Both houses have their own splendid legends and both are properties of the National Trust and open to the public. The ancestor of the historic family of Throckmorton was John de Throckmorton who died in 1130, but it was Sir John Throckmorton who during the reign of Henry IV married Eleanor, co-heiress of the Spinetos or Spinneys from whom she inherited the estate of the de Coton family, who began to build the present mansion.

The Throckmortons were a deeply devoted Roman Catholic family and as recusants suffered appalling losses for their faith during the reign of Elizabeth I. Most notably, Sir Thomas was imprisoned over and over again, deprived of property, heavily fined, yet never for one moment did he surrender his faith. So deep was his faith that they risked everything when, in 1585, they became involved in the Babington or Throckmorton Plot to murder Elizabeth and put Mary Queen of Scots on the throne. Two of the greatest treasures in their house are the chemise the Catholic queen wore at her execution, and the wonderful cope worked by Henry VIII's Queen Catherine of Aragon. Coughton Court still has its rooms for hiding priests who were celebrating secret masses, in one of which a Spanish leather altar was found.

Even more serious than their implication in the Babington plot was their dangerous involvement in the Gunpowder Plot of 1605, a plot to kill not only the king but also destroy both Houses of Parliament, in revenge for James the First's repression of the Roman Catholics. James had increased the penalties and fines for 'recusancy' and so incensed the Jesuit faction, many of whom had been expelled from Britain after the Throckmorton Plot, that several of them began preparations for their revenge. Although the Throckmortons were not themselves activists, Coughton Court was directly implicated when a group of wives and two priests gathered together in the gatehouse on that fatal night to await results.

Thomas, son of Sir Robert Throckmorton, cautiously decided to absent himself on that night of 5 November. He went abroad, lending the house to his brother-in-law, Sir Everard Digby. Some time after midnight the anxious listeners heard the sound of a galloping horse breaking the dramatic silence in the house. The messenger was Thomas Bates, servant of Sir William Catesby, a kinsman of the Throckmorton family, who brought the terrible news of the failure of the plot, on what was to be known as Guy Fawkes Night in the history of England. The guests dispersed and fled, making their escape to Holbeach Hall, one of Sir Everard Digby's properties in Staffordshire.

The family fortunes changed dramatically when Charles I came to the throne, for in 1642, the year of the outbreak of the Civil War, he conferred a baronetcy on Sir Robert Throckmorton.

One year later, Coughton Court was occupied by Parliamentary troops. In January 1644 Royalist troops heavily bombarded the family home, in spite of vain attempts by the inhabitants to sue for peace by hanging out white bed-clothes at the windows. The house was sacked, set on fire and badly damaged.

As if this misfortune were not bad enough, and in spite of great attempts at restoration of Coughton Court by Sir Francis, 2nd Baronet, more damage was done in 1688, when James II fled the country. On what has always traditionally been known as 'Running Thursday', a Protestant mob from Alcester pillaged the house, destroyed the newly built Catholic church and the entire east wing of the house which has never been replaced. It was not unil 1780 that the ruins were cleared away by Sir Robert, 6th Baronet, and from then on extensive restoration was carried out.

Not the least interesting part of the contents is surely the legendary and celebrated Thousand-Guinea Coat which has created a delightful legend linking Coughton Court with another family mansion in what was once Berkshire and is now Oxfordshire.

In the year 1690 the Manor of Buckland was held by Sir Francis Throckmorton, 2nd Baronet. In 1757 George Throckmorton built a gigantic mansion within a great park. It was from here that Sir John, 5th Baronet, made his celebrated wager with John Coxeter of Greenham Mills, Newbury.

The wager of 1,000 guineas was an enormous sum of money in 1811 when the challenge was made by Sir John. A displayed poster next to the coat in Coughton Court reads: 'Illustrative of Manufacturing Celerity to prove the possibility of Wool being manufactured into Cloth and made into a coat between sunrise and sunset on Tuesday 25th June 1811.'

Wool manufacturing had always been of great importance in Newbury since the time of the celebrated citizen Jack of Newbury. Berkshire was renowned for its sheep fairs and for its shepherds who drove flocks of sheep from Wales across the Berkshire Downs to Kingston upon Thames for sale. The export of wool and the import of cloth was prohibited and pressure of production had brought in steam, factories, and what John Coxeter as a great craftsman termed 'new-fangled machinery'. So confident was he of his mills and workmen as well as sheep and shepherds, that he never for one moment doubted his ability to make it and even engaged tailors to complete the coat.

John Coxeter started work at 5 a.m. with the shearing and slaughter of two live fat sheep and never ceased until eleven hours later. During that time the wool was washed clean, stubbed, spun and woven. When cloth it was also washed, fulled, trimmed and dyed a bright crimson colour as expressly desired by Sir John Throckmorton. At four o'clock precisely the tailors began their work on the cloth which, well before sunset, became the coat. The sheep were then roasted and served with 120 gallons of ale to the vast crowd who had watched all day. That night Sir John Throckmorton sat down to dinner in a fine and remarkable crimson hunting kersey coat.

John Coxeter, who was a popular and benevolent man to the poor of Newbury, kept the thousand guineas for a special occasion. It came three years later in 1814 when Napoleon was imprisoned on the Island of Elba, celebrated throughout England. John Coxeter invited all the poor people of Greenham, the nearby villages and Newbury itself to enjoy a unique plum pudding he had ordered to be made, twenty-four foot in length, borne on a waggon drawn by a team of horses. It was distributed on tables erected along Northbrook Street, the principal street of Newbury. For some time Sir John allowed his famous coat to be exhibited in Newbury Museum before bringing it to his home in Coughton Court where it remains for hundreds and thousands of annual visitors to see.

THE THYNNES

LONGLEAT

The magnificent Elizabethan mansion built by Sir John Thynne, always known as 'The Builder' has many legends and traditions, which is not surprising since it is one of the most haunted houses in England. Its line of succession has been three times challenged for a direct male heir. Even after a prophecy of doom to the whole family just seventy-five years ago, the line is still extant.

The prophecy of doom happened in 1916 and became a still existent legend. Violet Caroline, daughter of Sir Charles Marchant, Bt and wife of Thomas Henry (Thynne), 5th Marquess of Bath was sitting by the window in her room at Longleat House when she suddenly saw five swans flying low over the great lake, where for centuries the birds had nested. One of them suddenly broke away from the group, sped into the distance and disappeared. It did not return. After dinner that night she told her husband that it was a bad omen and forecast doom to the family. She told him also that now she feared for their son who was fighting during World War I in France. The next morning a telegram arrived briefly announcing the death of Alexander Thynne, Viscount Weymouth, killed in action. She never recovered from the blow and not long after left her husband a widower.

Just before her death she confirmed the doom she had already prophesied. She was herself psychic, not without reason in that haunted house, and asked one day why all the furniture and floor in the hall, still one of the finest features in the house, was covered with cloths. Her question caused astonishment to the others as they had seen nothing. That very night a serious fire broke out in the roof, threatening the entire mansion. Before the firemen and the staff rushed up to see what had to be done, the firemen covered the furniture and floor of the hall to prevent damage from falling slates, burnt timber and dust.

The magnificent mansion of Longleat in Wiltshire was originally an Augustinian priory housing the black canons, so called because of their gowns. The monks had been thrown out when Henry VIII ordered the dissolution of the monasteries and it had been bought by Sir John Thynne in 1540, who began to build a great house which unfortunately burnt down. He started all over again and after twelve years it emerged as one of the greatest houses in England with one hundred rooms and a Bath-stone frontage in the traditional English fashion. The house has been very little altered since, and stands proudly within its thousand acres of parkland and great lakes.

Longleat, attracting millions of visitors over the years, has now become a vast commercialized proposition, a huge studied 'entertainment complex' with its maze, pets corner, Longleat lions, safari park, train rides and boat trips, packed to capacity through the summer months by thousands of parents and children.

The name Thynne came from their ancestors the Bottrevilles, a Norman family who came to England to assist King John in his war against the barons. One of them called himself John o'th Inne to distinguish himself from the others. The Thynnes' first dramatic entry into history was probably the greatest challenge to their existence, when in 1682 Thomas Thynne, known as 'Tom o' Ten Thousand' because of his vast income, was assassinated, dying childless with no direct heir.

'Tom o' Ten Thousand' had become a close friend of the Duke of Monmouth, bastard son of Charles II by Lucy Walter. The Duke was a highly untrustworthy and potentially dangerous man and in a way played a major part in Thomas Thynne's murder by promising to use his influence to find him a second wife. The duke's choice was Elizabeth Ogle, daughter of the 11th Earl of Northumberland, who at the age of thirteen had been married to the heir of the Duke of Newcastle. He had died a year later, leaving her one of the most sought-after rich heiresses in the country. The Duke spoke of her beauty, her vivacity, and, flattering Thomas, suggested that as the wealthiest man in the country he might do well to consider her. Thomas's proposal was made and accepted. Elizabeth was then only fifteen, a red-haired beauty. In a bout of immense prodigality, Thomas prepared splendid apartments at Longleat for his bride and all her servants, careless of the expense. However, Elizabeth never came there and the marriage was never consummated since the bride fled to Holland.

She was immediately followed by Count Konigsmark, who had fallen deeply in love with her. He was only twenty-one, an adventurer who had led a notorious life all over Europe and had already made up his mind that the only way to win Elizabeth was to murder her husband 'Tom o' Ten Thousand'. He therefore hired three 'hit men', an impoverished Pole named Boroski, a Captain Vratz and a Lieutenant Stern, all mercenary adventurers who wandered about Europe and would do anything for money. Konigsmark ordered them to England to study Thomas Thynne's movements before they carried out the planned assassination.

On a dark Sunday night in February 1682 they saw Thynne leaving the Dowager Duchess of Northumberland's house near St James's Park, whose granddaughter was Thynne's wife. The three men followed his coach along Pall Mall where Stern pulled up in front of the coach and Vratz threatened the driver with a pistol, while Boroski thrust his blunderbuss into the coach and against his victim's body, firing five bullets into it in a cold-blooded murder. All three then took to their heels leaving Thynne to die. The link man and the watch had already raised the alarm and most curiously the Duke of Monmouth was the first to arrive at the scene of the murder.

An award of £200, then a substantial sum of money, was offered for their apprehension. Gibbon, one of the Duke of

Monmouth's retainers, gave information that led to the arrest of Konigsmark, who denied the charge. Acquitted by a bribed jury, he fled to Europe and was killed four months later fighting in Greece. The trial of the assassins became an international scandal. All three men were executed. Vratz made a last request that his body should be embalmed and placed on view to the public for fifteen days. Lady Elizabeth's third husband was Charles Seymour, 6th Duke of Somerset.

Two years later the title passed to Thomas Thynne's cousin Thomas (Thynne) created 1st Viscount Weymouth by Charles II. For many years after the Konigsmark sensation, he brought peace and tranquillity to Longleat. For twenty years his close friend Bishop Ken worked in the library now dedicated to him, and legend says his ghost visits it regularly each year. The bishop once refused to allow Nell Gwynne a lodging in the close at Winchester. When the appointment was to be made for Bath and Wells, Charles II, remembering the spirit Ken had shown, suddenly asked, 'Where is the good little man who refused his lodging to poor Nell?' And so Dr Ken became Bishop of Bath and Wells.

Like Thomas Thynne, the new Viscount left no direct heir, and so for the third successive time Longleat passed out of the direct line. The title went to a great-nephew, Thomas Thynne, 2nd Viscount Weymouth, who was a child in 1714 and did not go to Longleat until he came of age.

There is a story about the 2nd Viscount's sudden departure from Longleat. It appears that his stepfather, who had come to Longleat for a short stay, prolonged his visit so much that Viscount Weymouth told him one of them must go and he had decided to be the one. He never returned to Longleat but went to live in a small manor-house in the village of Horningsham.

This odd character was not at all popular with the villagers. He seemed to have had a very strong dislike for the extravagance and wealth which had marked the way of life of his ancestors. Yet, in spite of everything, he married twice and defied family tradition by being buried in Horningsham and not in the family vault at Longbridge Deverill where his wives lay. His son Thomas Thynne was created the 1st Marquess of Bath by George III in 1789, a title which continues to this day.

The 2nd Viscount Weymouth died and was buried with an astonishing secret that has become a family legend. Even today it remains an unsolved mystery. Did the viscount have a murder on his conscience? His first wife was Lady Louisa Cartaret from whom the family descends, a strikingly beautiful lady everywhere admired. The indomitable Sarah Jennings, Duchess of Marlborough wrote of her charm in her letters, and of her failure to understand why she had married Viscount Weymouth. An unknown man fell deeply in love with her and she with him. To make it easier for both of them, Lady Louisa hid him in Longleat House where they continued to meet until one day her husband, perhaps suspicious, made an unusual visit to Longleat and discovered them. A savage duel took place in a passage known as the Green Lady's Walk, ending in the death of the secret lover whose body the viscount buried under the cellar flagstones. There it lay for over two centuries until central heating was installed in Longleat, when the body of a man wearing jackboots was discovered under the cellar floors. Upon its exposure the body crumbled to dust. It is said that the spirit of the unhappy Lady Louisa haunts the passage still, no doubt the shock of the murder and her great grief hastening her own death.

It would be very interesting to know if Violet Caroline, the psychic wife of the 5th Marquess of Bath knew about this, for it was during his lifetime that central heating was installed at Longleat and the body found. She had concentrated upon the swans when she had prophesied a bad omen to the family and it would seem the discovery might have been made after her own tragic death. Since that time, however, there has been no further threat to the extinction of this most distinguished family, for there has been no record of the swans not returning to the lake. May they continue to remain and bring peace.

THE VENABLES-VERNON

THE DRAGON AND THE CHILD

The Venables and the Vernon families were two of the most illustrious Cheshire families. Both came over with William the Conqueror and for their services were given titles and vast lands in their county. Gilbert de Venables, supposed to be the younger brother of Stephen, Earl of Blois was granted the Barony of Kinderton. The Vernons were a Norman family who had considerable estates there and in Cheshire. It was a son, Richard de Vernon, who was created Baron of Shipbrooke by Hugh Lupus, Earl of Chester.

With each successive marriage with other families, estates and properties were naturally interchanged. It is interesting to note some of the forms of payment for buying and selling land during the centuries. In the reign of Edward II, Ralph de Vernon obtained lands consisting of many acres of meadow and forest, some of the lands covering rents of four pairs of gloves and eight arrows, as well as the advowsons of a chapel and church. Upon a marriage into the Savage family an even greater rent was exchanged for property, consisting of one pound of pepper, sixteen pairs of gloves, twenty barbed arrows and five roses.

The Vernons seem also to have been a remarkable family of mixture of characters, legitimate and illegitimate, notably perhaps the legendary Ralph de Vernon, Baron of Shipbrooke, known as 'Ralph the Olde' who was reputed to have lived to 150 years before, during and after the reign of Edward II. The history of Cheshire records numerous disputes during his lifetime, which is perhaps not surprising.

A more historically important member of the family was the Sir Richard de Vernon, 14th Baron of Shipbrooke, mentioned many times in Shakespeare's *Henry IV*, attainted and beheaded at Shrewsbury as a traitor to the new king in July 1403.

Much later in their history, the family had property in Shropshire, especially at Tong, seventeen miles north-east of Much Wenlock. Tong church has been compared to Westminster Abbey, if one can believe the American Consular who in 1868 stated it to be 'a little Westminster'. Its outstanding features are the magnificent tombs of the Vernons and the Great Bell of Tong. This was given to the church by Henry Vernon in 1518, has been recast twice in the centuries since and now weighs two tons. In the church porch is a list displaying the occasions when the bell is rung, including royal births and royal visits to Tong. It must also be rung for any visits made by the head of the Vernon family.

In their long family history it was inevitable amongst its many intermarriages there should be one with the equally illustrious and ancient family of Venables. Indeed it is surprising that nearly seven centuries passed before this occurred when Henry Vernon married into the Venables family and his son assumed the name and title of Venables-Vernon which is extant today under the title of Baron Vernon. The two families certainly met together in the dramatic rebellion against Henry IV led by Owen Glendower from Wales and 'Hotspur' Percy from the north; for Sir Richard de Venables met the same fate as Sir Richard de Vernon, both being attainted as traitors and beheaded in 1403 after the battle of Shrewsbury. Sir Richard de Venables also held the important position of Sheriff of Cheshire.

The Venables family were the sole possessors of

something unique both in legend and tradition. The story began when Sir Thomas de Venables, very early in the reign of Queen Elizabeth I, was challenged by Norroy, King of Arms during his visitation of Cheshire. To ensure the right of any person having a coat of arms, heralds were sent out by the College of Arms north and south of the river Trent to issue grants of arms to proven and rightful claimants which were permanently recorded in the college. These were entitled Visitations.

The very earliest coats of arms were those used in battles, the simplest of all coats of arms in design so that they were easily identifiable. As the centuries of arms and armour passed, coats of arms began to be used by all kinds of people, not necessarily of the nobility, but by landed gentry, lords of manors, knights and squires, until in the Tudor age the coats of arms were pompously and even ridiculously designed. Henry VIII was the first to see this as a fine way of raising money and he authorized the College of Arms to send out their Kings to make a detailed register of every coat of arms. Those that were justified were accepted and registered free of charge, all others had first to be accurately proved and payment made by them to be registered. Coats of arms had become for all these people a sign or token of a social position in society. Families were naturally proud of their coats of arms which brought in their many marriages, giving added importance which could be justifiably passed on to their children.

Thus it was during one of these Visitations of Cheshire that Norroy, King of Arms, visited Sir Thomas Venables, Baron of Kinderton in the County of Cheshire, not only to prove his claim to this title and coat of arms but to the unique crest above it. Sir Thomas claimed that centuries before one of his ancestors had fought and slain a dragon which was at that time eating a child. There have been many families whose ancestors have claimed to have killed dragons, but none has claimed to have killed a dragon while it was eating a child. Nevertheless it was a legend in Cheshire and a very proud tradition of the Venables family. Though the dragon and child had been an integral part of their coat of arms since the Venables came over with William the Conqueror, it now had to be registered or abandoned for ever. For the records of the College of Arms, Sir Thomas' pedigree and arms had to be proven by documents, seals or other evidence, so that he had an established right to both of them. The result of Norroy's visit was dutifully recorded in a long, complicated and pompously-worded grant of arms, in which was incorporated his chastisement of Sir Thomas Venables' misconduct in not previously informing the College of Arms. This was an act of discourtesy, warned Norroy, 'since his valiant worthiness might have been forgotten and sunk into oblivion.'

Norroy accepted Sir Thomas' simple shield of arms as two white bars on a blue shield, used for identification on the battle field and his title of Baron Kinderton granted him by William the Conqueror. His claim to the lordship of Moston and the addition of his dragon crest which he so proudly bore, was less convincing. This had been awarded to him by the Earl of Oxford's ancestors, who had granted this great honour to him because one of Sir Thomas' ancestors had purged Moston of a terrible dragon, who had for long ravaged the countryside, eaten cattle and even human beings until a Venables ancestor had set out to kill it and did so at the very moment it was actually devouring a child. The dragon was first shot through with an arrow and then killed by other weapons. Norroy, finally convinced of the validity to the crest, as well as all his heirs male, included it in the final full grant of arms authorized and signed by him on 30 October 1560.

When Henry Vernon married the niece of the last Baron of Kinderton, the family inherited all the estates. They proudly added the unique dragon crest to their own crest of a boar. It is an impressive and fearsome dragon holding between its powerful jaws the half-devoured body of a child. Surely a creature which even the worst of the Vernon enemies might well have hesitated being the first to attack, even in battle.

THE WAKES

HEREWARD THE WAKE

The extant family of Wake claims direct descent from England's great folk hero Hereward the Wake, or Wary, the celebrated outlaw and rebel of the Isle of Ely in Cambridgeshire. His heroic stand against William the Conqueror has become a legend, and was brought to life again by the Victorian novelist Charles Kingsley, though with more romance than history.

His parentage has been disputed by early authorities as have many of his exploits, but the most reliable gives him as the son of Leofric, Earl of Mercia, or of Bourne in Lincolnshire, a hard and unforgiving Saxon thegn, or nobleman; and of Ediva or Aedina, though others have stated that his mother was the saintly Lady Godiva, the legendary woman who rode naked through Coventry. Legend says that she had intended her second son Hereward to be a monk had she lived. Both the Ely and Croyland Chronicles give his mother as Ediva.

Hereward was a strong, athletic and venturesome boy with flaxen hair and one blue and one grey eye. He was rough and mischievous. Quite early on he became a leader of a band of youngsters who spent their time in horseplay, actions that soon began to annoy the inhabitants of Bourne and complaints were made to his father, then resident in London where he was an attendant to King Edward the Confessor. Leofric ordered him to leave the country and stay in the city. Hereward hated the change from the start and soon he was leading another gang whose exploits became a scandal. So outraged was his father that he applied to the king for a writ of outlawry to be issued against Hereward, which was granted. Hereward, with his friend and follower Martin Lightfoot, left England some time after 1062.

Legends had already begun, for before he vanished from London he was supposed to have gone north to Northumbria to his godfather Gilbert and was at once in trouble again. He is reported to have killed a white fairy bear which was attacking a princess, incurring his godfather's deep anger for he loved the bear. Hereward is next reported killing a giant in Cornwall, then fleeing to Ireland, where he fought in many campaigns on his horse Swallow, which he had either bought or captured. He was shipwrecked on his way to Flanders but survived. There he married Torfrida, a rich heiress, when news came to him of the conquest of England by Duke William, later king. One of the Conqueror's first actions was to deprive all landowners of their lands and hand them over to his own followers. Thus all the shares were divided and given to French-speaking barons and prelates who in turn repaid the king with knights fees.

The Domesday book gives no mention of lands held in England by Hereward's father, though he held three small estates in Bourne, Lincolnshire. His arrival in the village was horrific for over the doorway of his own house he saw his brother's decapitated head. It was nightfall and he and Martin Lightfoot found a shocked and mourning village. They were told that a party of Normans had plundered and pillaged his house, killed his brother, and were celebrating their deeds in his hall with a great party. The author of the *Gesta Herewardi,* the most authentic of the commentaries, otherwise called *The Deeds of the Famous, Exile and Warrior,* gives a graphic account of the party, describing how Hereward made his servant dress and arm him putting his mailshirt under his tunic and hiding his helmet under a black coat. The deadly sword he had acquired called Brainbiter finally slew fourteen of the

Normans, unable to find their own weapons. When morning came his young brother's head was replaced by fourteen bloody Norman heads. As the news spread so did the revolt and before long Hereward was at the head of yet another band of warriors ready for revenge and to die for it.

News of Hereward's deed spread rapidly amongst the Danes and Saxons. Anxious as he was to deal with the Norman invaders, he soon learnt that there were other rebels in Ely who were prepared to join up with him. It is at this point, when Hereward sets out to find the other rebels, that actual history takes over from legend in the main. The principal authorities are the *Anglo-Saxon Chronicle*, the *Chronicle of Croyland Abbey* in Lincolnshire, the twelfth-century *Liber Elenis* or *Ely Book*, and the contemporary Hugh Candidus, even though these accounts vary.

The Conqueror's determination to replace Saxon principal officers, especially those of the Church, was marked by the appointment of a Norman to Peterborough Abbey, one of the most valuable in England. The newly appointed man was Thorold of Fecamp in Normandy, who at that time was Abbot of Malmesbury and, according to William of Malmesbury's *Chronicle*, was 'a harsh and stern man, who was translated to Peterborough Abbey on the death of Brand, the previous incumbent'.

Hereward, informed of this, decided to 'sack the abbey and burn the town' and set out to do it before Thorold arrived there. The monks put up a strong defence, incensed that such a plan should be carried out by one of their own tenants. The wealth of the abbey was incalculable and not to be taken, as William of Malmesbury wrote, 'by one Hereward and his gang of robbers.'

Hereward, repulsed at all points by the defending monks, at once set fire to all their buildings until the flames spread so fast that his band were able to enter and begin the massive plunder from what had always been known as the Golden Borough. The Danes with him were even more ruthless in seizing treasures, many of which they took back to Scandinavia and which have never been recovered.

Hereward, sated with loot and satisfied with his revenge, wisely decided to prepare for what he knew would be an inevitable retaliation by King William. At the time, however, the king was far too concerned with the resistance in Scotland and Wales to deal with an isolated rebel like Hereward. Thus it was not until 1070 that he moved his forces to mount his first attack on Ely Abbey where Hereward had entrenched himself and his followers.

In those times the Isle of Ely was described in the *Ely Book*: 'Eel Island is called that by the vast number of eels you can catch in the marshes there.' In fact such was their abundance that the monks drew an annual rental of almost 173,000 eels in the thirteenth century. Its vast area of marshland and scarcity of tracks had always assured its safety from attack. The king had set out with a considerable force, not even imagining that it would be the first of three campaigns in which he would be twice defeated and only victorious in the third because of the treachery of the monks and not because of his military skill.

In his *History of England* G.M. Trevelyan wrote: 'The military drama of the contest closed with the vast operation conducted by William against the Isle of Ely defended by Hereward. Hereward was a man of the Fenland district with a genius for amphibious warfare in that difficult country.'

All the early writers are in confusion about this first campaign, but the *Gesta* gives a terrifying account of it. In a way it resembles Napoleon's retreat from Moscow, the army finally beaten by nature, substituting the fen marshes for Russian snow. It is a brilliant piece of narrative and was written only about fifty years after the campaign had ended. The writer even states that he personally remembered seeing the end of it. '... countless attackers were drowned in the fen marshes without even coming to blows with the defenders, so that even today many bodies in rotting armour are still dragged out of the depths. I myself have seen not a few of them.'

Having conquered almost a whole country, the king was infuriated by such a defeat inflicted by one man. Persuaded by his council to make a second attempt, he ordered a causeway to be built from Aldreth to Ely Abbey and to engage a French sorceress to turn the tables against Hereward by witchcraft.

Unknown to the king, Hereward, certain there would be another attack, decided to act as a spy and find his way into William's camp. On his way he met a potter whom he persuaded to change clothes with him and hand him his wares, no doubt for money. The potter agreed, and so disguised Hereward was able to enter the camp and discover the plans for a second attack. This took place eight days later. A tower had been built on the causeway from which the witch was to start her incantations and spells. The Normans began the assault by force, wholly unaware that Hereward and his men were hidden in the marshes, hearing the witch shrieking out her curses upon them as they crept across the edge of the swamp and into the reeds to which they set fire. The flames travelled faster than the soldiers on the causeway and panic broke out as smoke poured across the causeway and Hereward's men fired their arrows into the Normans. The screaming and now terrified witch was the first to leap from the burning wooden tower to die. The slaughter was even greater than in the first attack, forcing William to withdraw 'cursing all the way back to his camp.'

Fortunes changed in a different way for the king when his spies, able to find their way into Ely Abbey, threatened severest punishment to the frightened monks unless they helped the king's army to enter by another way. The monks, wearied by the struggles, agreed to lead the Normans into their abbey by a secret path if they were guaranteed their safety and the treasures of their house. One of them, however, betrayed his brothers by telling Hereward the news, thus enabling him to escape with a few of his rebels. On 27 October 1071 Ely Abbey, converted into a fortress by Hereward, fell to William.

History ended there and legend took over when Hereward, like Robin Hood, sought safety in the dense woods of Northamptonshire. Almost from that moment confusion about his whereabouts and death began, continuing down to this day through all the different accounts. Indeed his own legend was supplanted by that of Robin Hood, though whereas the latter is but a shadowy historic figure the existence of Hereward is not to be doubted.

If the treacherous monks believed that the king would keep his promise they were very soon deceived. The most important were either imprisoned, their eyes torn out, or their hands and feet cut off. Though the monks kept their estates he imposed such heavy fines on them that they were forced to sell their treasures to him, and when the heavy fines were increased they became penniless and were cast out.

According to one account, Hereward went to Rockingham Forest on the outskirts of Northamptonshire, now Cambridge. There was a huge price on his head, whether captured alive or dead, for the king had mobilized all the shires. The pursuit had begun almost before Hereward reached the forest. It was said that he had had the horseshoes reversed on his great horse Swallow, but this is most unlikely. Hereward and his men emerged once to mount an attack on Stamford but were forced to retreat, and returning to the forest they became hopelessly lost and desperate.

At that moment, it is said, St Peter sent them a wolf to

show them the way and as darkness fell lighted candles appeared on every tree and on every man's shield, burning steadily irrespective of how the wind blew, guiding them deeper into the forest and to safety. From then onwards the mystery of Hereward's end deepens and is still unresolved in spite of the various extant records. Kingsley tells us that he was reinstated by the king through the medium of a powerful woman who assured him that he would be honoured and at liberty if he forsook his wife Torfrida and married her; a somewhat sordid and unconvincing story.

That King William did in fact forgive him and restored his land and estates in Bourne is not improbable, but that he actually accompanied the king back to Normandy to suppress the rebels of Maine early in 1073, two years after the surrender of Ely Abbey and Hereward's flight, is totally improbable. If indeed the king forgave Hereward, his Norman subjects never did. It is said that while Hereward was waiting to swear his oath of allegiance to the king, the Norman knights persuaded one of their strongest, named Ogger, to pick a quarrel with Hereward and force him to fight a duel. Hereward, though provoked, was in no mood to fight until he lost his temper and severely wounded Ogger. The knights then rushed to the king to tell him that Hereward had started the fight. He is supposed to have been sent to prison in Bedford.

Another story is that he and his men were surrounded in Rockingham Forest and murdered. But according to the *Gesta* he was taken back by the king and recovered his estates. 'And these he enjoyed for many years after serving King William faithfully and also devotedly pleasing his friends and fellow-countrymen until in the end he died in peace. On whose soul may God have mercy. Amen.' One might reasonably be surprised that such a born rebel could ever die in peace or as *The Chronicle of Croyland Abbey* records, though two centuries later: 'Hereward, by his special choice was buried by

Torfrida's side in Croyland Abbey church and that his lands in Bourne then passed to his unmarried daughter ...'

One day perhaps the manner of Hereward's death will be revealed; but this great medieval outlaw became a legend in ballads and songs sung in the taverns of Lincolnshire and far beyond for almost two centuries after his death. In the high drama of the Norman Conquest, he was the principal actor in the heroic siege of the Isle of Ely which lasted for as long as was possible between a small band of Saxon rebels against the powerful Norman army under its ruthless king. Such a struggle might have gone on for a much longer time had not the monks betrayed him. So cherished was the memory of this man in Lincolnshire that Roger of Wendover wrote of men still making a pilgrimage to a wooden fortress in the fens known to them as Hereward's Castle but which is no longer there.

It was customary in early times for many distinguished families, such as the Bourchiers, Staffords and Heneages, to have their own badge or crest. The most curious of these badges was the knot. These were of silk or cord intertwined in various shapes, constituting a small but distinct class of badge. It is therefore most interesting to find that the distinguished Wake family have today as their crest an intricate knot, on the proud assumption that they are directly descended from Hereward the Wake, and that they attribute the knot to him. He is still further commemorated in the crest of Ely County Council. Another and less intricate knot is the Wake and Ormonde Knot.

THE WALLACES

A FOLK HERO

Very little is known of the thirteenth-century family of Wallace, and much of what is written about it is conjectural, but one member of it became a legendary figure still known not only in Scotland but also in

England. It was the minstrel 'Blind Hary' who, in the fifteenth century, composed his many volumes of poetry and prose about the war of independence between Scotland and England in which Sir William Wallace was the hero. Had this not been written, it is possible that history would have overlooked the exploits and legends concerning Wallace.

Like Hereward the Wake, William Wallace has become a folk hero of great importance. Both men were dedicated to their struggle against suppression by another country no matter what the odds against them. Both were outlawed, hunted down with a price on their heads. Both were forced into hiding in forests through years of legendary exploits. However Hereward the Wake, though probably murdered, escaped the brutal and horrific execution carried out on the captured Sir William Wallace by the English in 1305.

Various accounts have been written of the Wallace family, even their name has varied from Waley to le Waley (the Welshman). They were not of the nobility but were landed gentry with estates in either Ayrshire or Strathclyde and William's father was dead by 1297, William being either the second or third son.

It was a savage age of divided loyalties both in Scotland and England, brought to a head by Edward I, the Hammer of the Scots, who waged war with them throughout his reign.

The king, asserting his Saxon rights to the overlordship of Scotland which were renounced by the Scottish king Balliol, marched into Scotland, seized the stone of Scone and brought it back to London where it is today in Westminster Abbey. He left a considerable part of his army in Scotland to control a naturally hostile and dangerous country. A large number of these men were mercenaries of the worst sort who had massacred most of the inhabitants of Berwick on their way into Scotland. They now wandered about the countryside, pillaging and looting the farmsteads and villages, insulting the Scots who were often unable to resist. There was one man who did however. He was Sir William Wallace.

This 'guerilla chief of genius' as Trevelyan called him in his *History of England,* 'was a tall man of iron strength, who suddenly appears on the page of history as if from nowhere.' The dramatic start of his meteoric and legendary career began when he slew the English sheriff in Lanark, Scotland. One of the first of many legends says it was because the sheriff had killed Wallace's sweetheart or wife, though there is no record of this in 'Blind Hary's' book. 'Blind Hary' says that he was tall of stature, 6′ 9″, and massive of frame with a clear countenance and a cheerful manner, a pleasing aspect but a fierce expression. If we accept Fordun's statement that William's father died in 1297 he must now have been aged between twenty and twenty-one, though this too is speculative. What is neither speculative nor legendary is the fact that he had a dedicated and passionate hatred of the English oppressors. His loyalty was to his country and to no one else. There were already stories of his many skirmishes with the hated 'southerners' in which he always seemed to emerge victorious.

His position was at that time an isolated one since Robert Bruce, once a claimant to the Scottish throne, had now joined the English overlords, together with many Scottish nobles and earls who had sworn allegiance to Edward I, believing and trusting that by doing so they would not lose all their lands and estates. The massacre of Berwick, however, incensed Wallace and many others, especially the peasants, who flocked to him as a possible leader against the hated English. Gradually Wallace formed a band of mostly violent and revengeful men, especially those small landowners who had had their farms pillaged and even destroyed. Wallace began their training at once. He was himself, it was said, a fine archer, and the men followed him like sheep.

With this band of badly armed but resolute and courageous men Wallace stormed the English stronghold of Stirling Castle in 1297. The English were driven out by this totally unexpected attack from a badly accoutred army of desperate men who now gave Wallace the title of 'Guardian of Scotland'. King Edward, infuriated by this defeat, headed north at once with a powerful army to deal with Wallace whom he now outlawed as a traitor. Wallace's victory brought thousands of men to his army, burgesses, lairds and men of the nobility flocked to his side. With a now considerable army Wallace prepared to do battle with Edward, sure that victory would come to them again since they had had some eighteen months to plan for the inevitable return of the English. They took up their stand on 11 September at Abbey Craig (where the Wallace Memorial now stands).

Confusion abounds about the whole of the battle amongst both English and Scottish chroniclers; but after scoring a number of victories over the English, Wallace led his army southwards to invade England through Galloway and Carlisle into Cumberland, before starting to return home, where at Falkirk their army was routed.

Wallace was ill-equipped against the heavily armed, well-trained and disciplined English cavalry and infantry and their redoubtable archers. Thousands of his men were slaughtered, many of them deserted, especially the nobles who thought it wiser to flee rather than fight and risk losing all their lands and their lives as well. Of the very few who left the battlefield alive one was Sir William Wallace. From that moment, and for the next seven years, history ceases and legends begin which have multiplied ever since.

Like all outlaws, such as Hereward the Wake and Robin Hood, Sir William took to hiding in forests, deserted by all. An enormous price was placed on his head, dead or alive, as he struggled to survive without money or provisions and alone. It was almost two centuries before 'Blind Hary' wrote his enormous poem, *The Acts and Deeds of Sieur William Wallace* published in Scotland, in which he lamented bitterly over the failure of Scotland to honour such a man when other nations, especially England, had so dishonoured him. It has been acknowledged by many writers that Hary's poem is a mixture of fact and fiction, yet he is decidedly sincere in his details of characters, condemnatory or not. He tells, for example, that Wallace had once killed a man who could not keep up with the rest of his army on the march '... some deal it good and others deem it ill', writes Hary, a verdict which could apply to another of his stories. This was when a boy and two English heralds were sent to Wallace from King Edward. The visit ended by Wallace killing the boy and sending the two heralds back, one blinded, the other with his tongue cut out. Of Wallace's slaying of the English sheriff at Lanark he tells us that Wallace was dressed in May-time green on the day, flaunting his longsword over his shoulder and his dagger at his side, being jeered by the English soldiers until the murder happened before their eyes.

In a more romantic vein, 'Blind Hary' tells us that there was a price not only on Wallace's head but on anyone who harboured him and that a lady who had done so was sentenced to death. Hary adds 'that Wallace wept hot tears every time he told the story for he had loved the lady'. The poet adds that even 'such lusty payne' did not weaken him for war. It seems that Wallace, intent upon securing aid for the Scottish cause, set out first for Norway under a safe conduct given to him by King Haakon V. On the voyage his ship was attacked by Red Rover, a famous pirate whom he defeated and then entered into a warm friendship with this much-feared man. From Norway, Wallace is said to have visited France where he was welcomed at the court of King Philip the Fair. Later he was challenged to fight a lion. After arrogantly stating that he would fight nothing that did not wear armour, he put on a cloak and slew the animal with a single sword-blow. He then asked the spectators 'if there were any other dogges they wanted slayne?'

King Philip is said to have written a letter beseeching King Edward to have a six-month truce with Scotland, which was ignored. He also wrote to the Pope in Rome 'begging him to show favour to Our Beloved Sir William le Walleys.' It is interesting to note that Wallace had personally chosen this title. Whether help in any way was given or not, Wallace was back in Scotland to assist Robert Bruce, the newly accepted 'Guardian of the Kingdom of Scotland', who had invaded Cumberland from Galloway to lure the English armies back once more to Scotland, confident another battle might settle the liberty of Scotland for ever.

King Edward, again disturbed by the arrival of Wallace in action, offered a huge award for his capture, dead or alive. He added that there would be no mercy shown unless he surrendered absolutely. Wallace, however, protected only by the love and devotion of the poor people was as elusive as mercury, either in battle or 'skulking' in the Forest of Salkirk. Hary the poet becomes so immersed in his musing that it is as if he were in the forest with Wallace, hungry and lonely, wondering if God is angry with him for his unceasing battle for Scottish freedom. He tells us that Wallace then fell asleep under an oak tree and it was there that five men, aware of the price on his head, pounced on him. Wallace 'leapt up like a verytable Samson and killed them all before catching all the food for them carried by a boy, ravenously eating'.

In the last two books of his poem Hary departs increasingly from the truth, almost to the point of ridicule as when he tells us that at the meeting of the English queen with Wallace at St Albans in England she was so impressed by the chivalry of this man that she requested him to be presented to her. Separating from his followers, Wallace, in full armour, stepped forward to meet her, preventing her kneeling to him by taking her in his arms and most gallantly kissing her. Then after drinking with her from a loving-cup he steadfastly declined her implorations that such a chivalrous knight as he should swear fealty to King Edward. She returned 'sadly to her king for she was assured all trew Scotts would not have found his refusal distasteful to them from a man who was a monument of worship, wit, manhood and governance of freedom and truth.' Since Wallace had never been so far into England and there was no English Queen at the time, one must accept that there is more legend and fiction than historic fact in Hary's vast poem.

Suddenly legend ceases and history reappears for the last time when Wallace was betrayed by a Scot and arrested on 3 August 1305 in Glasgow 'where he lay in bed with his whore.' From there, under very heavy guard because of his immense strength, Wallace was brought to London and to trial in Westminster Hall. Even in that savage time the brutality of the English jurisprudence was appalling in its final judgment on a brave man. Before the Lord Mayor and a great company of nobles and eminent citizens, he was seated on an improvised throne and a laurel wreath was set on his head, a mocking jest to the man who had once said he would one day wear a crown in that very hall. It was a show trial. Wallace was condemned by long statements about his treachery and treason, before he was sentenced to death. He spoke only once, denying the charge of treason because he had never acknowledged King Edward as his sovereign.

On 22 August 1305, before a huge crowd, Wallace suffered the full agony of the horrific execution of being hanged, drawn and quartered. This was the first time this punishment had been carried out against an outlaw since 1284. He was bound hand and foot, wrapped in a bullskin and placed on a hurdle harnessed to horses, who dragged his body through the streets of the city to Smithfield, where the slaughterhouses were. There he was hanged, cut down alive, disembowelled and then beheaded, his head held high for the public to see. His body was then hacked into quarters and sent to Newcastle, Berwick, Stirling and Perth to remind the Scots of what would happen to any outlaw. His head was then borne aloft on a spike to be placed on London Bridge, also as a warning to any outlaw.

Ballads, songs and chapbooks multiplied about Wallace. His name passed into lasting legends: idolized by the Scots as the hero he was, regarded as a ruthless, cold-blooded murderer by the English, he was finally accepted by both as an outstanding folk hero of all time. For all Wallace's ferocity as a formidable guerrilla leader, the strangest thing is that it was the Scots who suffered far more than the English during the following three centuries of ceaseless Border warfare, for no one came to take his place.

Two years after the execution King Edward died, as ruthless and cruel as his enemy had been; he has not passed into legend as his implacable enemy has.

The splendid brass of Sir Ivo Fitzwaryn on a wall of St. Peter and St. Paul's church in Wantage, Oxfordshire (formerly Berkshire)

The Elizabethan manor at Charlecote Park, Warwickshire, in which Shakespeare was flogged by order of Sir Thomas Lucy

Part of the remains of Godstow nunnery near Oxford, where Fair Rosamund's tomb so enraged the bishop of Lincoln

The beautiful wooden bust of King Bladud, reputedly carved by Grinling Gibbons

Aldworth church in Berkshire, showing some of the vandalized de la Beche giants lying on their slabs

The bowl known as the *Luck of Muncaster*, given to Sir John Pennington by Henry VI, with a picture of the king holding it. Courtesy of Muncaster Castle Estate Office

The secluded setting of the ruins of Minster Lovell Hall on the edge of Wychwood forest, with the church close by

The famous Newbury coat made for Sir John Throckmorton on display at Coughton Court, Warwickshire

The tomb of Anthony Forster, Amy Robsart's steward, in the Oxfordshire church of St. Michael

Buckland Abbey in Devon, which Sir Francis Drake purchased in 1582

Drake's drum, which accompanied Sir Francis on his voyages, now on view in Buckland Abbey

The Tristan Stone standing on the road between Fowey and Castle Dore, where King Mark had his fortress

2 *Mystery Legends*

THE DE LA BECHES

A FAMILY OF GIANTS

In all the legends and myths of folklore some of the very earliest were of giants and fairies. Whilst there are many people today who believe in fairies, there are only a few who believe in giants. The legends of the Celts, of course, concern ancestral giants who were responsible for lifting the massive stones of Stonehenge in Wiltshire into place and also those of St Michael's Mount in Cornwall and the Wrekin in Shropshire.

There are also a few celebrated individual giants. Some named by Geoffrey of Monmouth, the twelfth-century chronicler include Gogmagog who gave his name to Gogmagog's Leap in Plymouth, Devon. The two giants Gog and Magog of Guildhall, London, are famous. Perhaps the best-known individual giants are the Cerne Abbas Giant of Dorset, 35 metres long wielding a heavy club 36.5 metres long, and the Long Man of Wilmington in Kent, 70 metres high, who holds in either hand staves as long as himself.

This very special type of folk hero was greatly feared in pagan times. Many were cruel, some were kind, acting as guardians of sheep, most were stupid, easily outwitted by men like the celebrated Cornishman, Jack the Giant-killer. With the birth of Christianity it was inevitable that giants should fade even from legends, though names linger on.

Both Carn Boscawen and Carn Galvert in Cornwall claim a Giant's Pulpit, whose occupant protected the people in return for meals of sheep. One interesting giant is the Somerset giant Gabbist who took on the Devil for a wager, lost the battle and was thrown into the Bristol Channel by his victor. As long as such stories exist giants live on in legend.

It is therefore unique to find a family of nine giants such as those whose stone effigies in Aldworth church are one of the richest collections of such monuments in the British Isles. The family represented is that of de la Beche, who in the course of just under a century became crown figures attached to the courts of Edward I, II and III in a military capacity. They had a manor and a castle at Aldworth, and another castle at Beaumys near Reading, both in Berkshire. They also held vast lands and great wealth, but might well have passed into oblivion had not Nicholas, last of the male line, had the stone effigies built to commemorate his ancestors.

The legend of this distinctive family began long ago when the local people gave nicknames to four of the family, as John Long, John Strong, John Everafraid and John Neverafraid; they, with the other five, are known to this day as the Sleeping Giants of Aldworth. Their fame was increased when Queen Elizabeth I insisted on paying a visit to see for herself these strange figures, today unfortunately badly mutilated and defaced. Three knights are under beautifully carved canopies against the north wall, while two knights and a lady are under similar canopies against the south wall. Another knight together with his lady lie on table tombs under arcade arches between the nave and the aisle. All the knights are cross-legged which has all too often been said to indicate going on one of the Crusades.

The names of the stone effigies are all conjectural, but as in all legends the facts are a matter of dispute. Nicholas de la Beche is recorded as being granted the privilege of crenellating his castle by Henry III. His son Robert was knighted by Edward I in 1278. His effigy is probably the one at the entry to the church by the north door. His son was the first of four Johns and had three sons, Nicholas, Philip, and the second John who married Isabella. Their son was the third John who married Joan. It is quite impossible to distinguish any of them and the confusion of identity of the effigies and the dubbed nicknames begins. Sir Philip, over seven feet in stature, was a real giant, easily recognized by the stone dwarf crouched at his feet emphasizing in death as in life the stature of his master. Philip and his dwarf were inseparable, especially when he was in attendance at the Court of Edward II where his great height could be noticed.

The most interesting features of these effigies are the reclining ones, seeming to denote either restlessness or adding a casual grace since they do not lie flat on their backs with eyes closed as do the majority of effigies. There is the lone figure of a lady, her mantle falling in vertical folds, and a knight and his lady. They are Sir John and his wife Isabella, particularly interesting because in 1871 an important discovery was made during local excavations. This was an ancient silver seal inscribed S'Isabella de la Beche', engraved with a trefoil cusped and roseated like the canopies over the six effigies in St Mary's church. Her effigy is headless and her body mutilated. At her feet is a sleeping hound, a sign of devotion; her husband John's body is also mutilated and lies beside her on the altar tomb.

The inability to identify the giants with accuracy except for Philip, was clearer to Colonel Richard Symonds, serving in Charles I's army during the civil wars. It would seem these sleeping giants would never have awakened such local and public interest had he not happened to visit St Mary's church, Aldworth. He was so excited by what he saw there on 2 May 1644 that he made several notes and fine drawings of these remarkable stone effigies. These drawings are preserved in the British Library (Harley MS 965). He was certainly the first man to record details about them and make positive identification of the most mysterious of the giants, John Everafraid, as he was known by the locals who dubbed him that. The Colonel's notes state:

> Aldworth vulgo Alder. In ye E. ende of ye S. yle did hang a table fairly written in parchments of all ye names of ye family of de la Beche, but ye Earle of Leicester coming with ye Queen Elizabeth in progresse, took it downe to show it her, and it was never broughte again. Ye common People call ye statue under ye outside of ye church, John Everafraid, and say further that he gave his soule to ye Divil and that if ever he was buried either in Church or Churchyarde, so he was buried under the Church Wall under an Arche.

The Colonel added that he believed him to be the oldest member of the family, but his belief cannot be substantiated. What is most interesting is that one of his drawings has a caption below it saying, 'The people call this statue John Strong.' There seems evidence therefore that the four giants named by their suffixes may have been given them by the people in the very beginning. This particular sketch gives no clue as to which one was Strong, Long or Neverafraid. Sir Nicholas, for example, was Lieutenant of the Tower and guardian of the Black Prince, imprisoned for being remiss in either collecting, or failing to send in, money to the treasurer of Edward III. Before his own death Sir Nicholas decided he would have stone effigies carved of them all to be placed in the church for perpetuity. This was accordingly carried out and has resulted in yet another mystery for he included his own effigy in the nine figures.

All traces of John Everafraid have disappeared. The arch under which he and his stone effigy were buried was either destroyed or blocked up or both. Perhaps the Devil decided all this when he received John Everafraid's soul.

The blame for all this enduring mystery and confusion must rest securely on the shoulders of the Earl of Leicester when he brought his beloved Queen Elizabeth from Ewelme to Aldworth to see the giants. She rode pillion on the earl's horse over what were very bad roads, and it was indeed a great honour to a great family. But what did the earl do with the list of names of the effigies? One day perhaps it will turn up and solve forever all the problems of the exact identification of the giants which have confused historians and many thousands of visitors alike.

It is fortunate indeed that the precious seal of the headless Lady Isabella de la Beche was not discovered until two centuries after Leicester's visit to Aldworth church, for he would have undoubtedly presented it to his queen. This exquisite fragment of silverwork, perhaps the finest of its kind in the country, was sold to Reading Museum where it is now on show to the public.

THE LOVELS

THE WARS OF THE ROSES

The fifteenth-century Minster Lovell Hall, the ruins of which are now in the protective care of English Heritage is visited by thousands of people each year. These romantic ruins in the beautiful Windrush valley, backed by a line of trees, all that remains of the once important Wychwood Forest, lie between the Oxfordshire towns of Burford and Witney and were once the home of the ill-fated Lovel family. The mansion is a splendid example of medieval domestic architecture, exemplified by its west tower, its fifty-foot-high stately banqueting-hall with central fire-place, its finely detailed large windows and vaulted passage. Outside is the medieval pigeon-loft or dovecote complete with nesting-boxes. It was built by the 7th Baron

William Lovel between 1431 and 1442 on the site of a small Norman priory attached to Ivry Abbey, to commemorate which the Baron preceded the name by 'Minster'. He lies in the aisleless cruciform church in a splendid fifteenth-century alabaster tomb.

This ancient Norman family came to England with William the Conqueror. Legend has it that one of the family's ancestors had such a dangerous and violent temper that he was nicknamed Lupus, the Wolf. His son, inheriting his father's temper, was known as Lupellus, or Little Wolf. This name became Lupel and finally Lovel or Lovell. The 1st Baron was created in 1299 and inherited vast lands in Northamptonshire. John, 5th Baron, was created a Knight of the Garter by Richard II. Their wealth increased by successive marriages to co-heiresses of other celebrated families until William, 7th Baron, built the great mansion he lived in for twenty-five years.

Suddenly this accumulation of wealth and high honours was seriously threatened by the outbreak of the War of the Roses in 1399 when Henry IV usurped the throne from the Yorkist Richard II, the wars ending with the final extinction of the Plantagenet line and the creation of the Tudor dynasty. The Lovels, loyal Yorkists, were soon involved, lucky to survive at all. It was in the reign of Richard III (1483–5) that Francis, succeeding as 9th Baron Lovel, was elevated to Viscount, receiving from the king the highest honours in the land, including the appointments of Constable of Wallingford Castle and Chief Butler of England. It was also the beginning of the extinction of the Lovell line and the extraordinary mystery of the legend of Minster Lovell Hall.

Very soon the Lancastrians had issued the insinuating and widely spread couplet which cost the writer his head:

> When the Cat, the Rat, and Lovel the Dog.
> All ruled England under the Hog.

The hog was Richard III, the cat was Catesby, the rat

Ratcliff and the dog Lovel. Catesby's badge was a white cat spotted with black, wearing a gold collar; Lovel's crest on his coat of arms was a silver wolf-dog, an allusion to his ancestor's nickname Lupus; it had a gold coronet around its neck. He fought at Bosworth, was lucky enough to keep his head where the king had lost his, fled first to Lancashire then to France to Margaret Duchess of Burgundy, the widowed sister of the last king Richard III, where he agreed to support the cause of the pretender Lambert Simnel. In May 1487 he landed in England at the head of 2,000 badly armed German mercenaries but failed to find supporters for the Yorkist cause. He was defeated at the battle of Stoke and once again escaped. There are various versions of what happened next, but the most reliable is that of Francis Bacon in his *History of Henry VII* (1622)

> Of the Lord Lovel there went a report that he fled and swam over the Trent on horseback, but could not recover the further side by reason of the steepness of the bank, and was drowned in the river. But another report leaves him not there but that he lived long after it in a cave or vault.

Henry VII reacted swiftly to the Lovel misfortunes by the Act of Attainder, under which he confiscated for the Crown all the vast family estates and wealth, most especially Minster Lovell Hall, 'that mansion inferior to none in my kingdom.'

Under the attainder the four Baronies of Lovel, Holand, Deincourt and Grey of Rotherfield went into abeyance. The Barony of Lovel and Holand became invested in the Earl of Egmont.

In 1562 it became necessary to secure evidence of Lovel's death for the legal disposal of his property. A jury established a verdict that he had escaped beyond the sea and died abroad, but this was not based on actual evidence. There were many people living near Minster

Lovell who were convinced that he had secretly found his way back to hide in his home until it would be safe to emerge. The legend spread beyond the county that somewhere he was alive, in spite of the fact that the great abandoned mansion became more and more ruined. Then a very remarkable thing happened, which certainly strengthened the legend that Lovel had indeed once returned.

A letter written by William Cowper, then clerk of the Parliament, recorded a singularly disquieting piece of information from his home in Hertingfordbury Park which had been related to him by John Manners, third Duke of Rutland.

> Sir, I met t'other day with a memorandum I had made some years ago perhaps not unworthy of notice. You remember that Lord Bacon, in his *History of Henry the Seventh* about Lord Lovel's escape … Apropos of this on the 6th May 1728, the present Duke of Rutland stated in my hearing that about twenty years before, viz. in 1708, upon occasion of laying a new chimney at Minster Lovell there was discovered a large vault underground in which was the entire skeleton of a man as having been sitting at a table which was before him, with a book, paper, pen etc; in another part of the room lay a cap, all much moulded and decayed. Which the family and others, judged to be the lord Lovel whose exit has hitherto been so uncertain.

The mystery of Lovel's death has never been explained. The slender evidence available suggests that he managed to return to his home where a trusted servant might have hidden him in the room where he was found sitting, but it will never be known if the servant, who alone had the key, died or perhaps betrayed his master by leaving him in this living tomb to starve to death.

An even stranger story is of the appearance a while later of a man known as Rustling Jack, who claimed to be the viscount's former valet and who, after the fatal battle of Stoke, had fled to Spain. He said that the Lovel treasure was also hidden with its master. Four people, one a monk, set out to find this treasure, and armed with picks and shovels they found the secret chamber where the skeleton of Viscount Lovel sat at the table. Whether they found the treasure will never be known, but before their horrified eyes the skeleton suddenly crumbled to a pile of dust.

THE OXENHAMS

THE WHITE BIRD

From the time of Henry III (1216–72) until the end of the nineteenth century the Oxenham family lived in the area of Devon between Okehampton and Exeter. This area included Zeal Monachorum where the Oxenham Manor was; St Andrew's church, South Tawton, where a rich heiress, Margaret Oxenham, was supposed to have been stabbed to death; and South Zeal where in the year 1700 they sold their manor-house to one of the Hoare family and bought the Great House from the Burgoyne family, which is now the Oxenham Arms, an attractive inn.

The Oxenham Omen has become one of the most mysterious legends in folklore history, unfortunately revealed to the general public first in a noticeably inaccurate version in Charles Kingsley's novel *Westward Ho!* On its publication, the Revd S. Baring-Gould severely criticized the tradition of the White Bird, or bird with a white breast, whose visitation to a member of the Oxenham family came as a death warning. A similar omen of a white bird on Salisbury Plain bringing death to a Bishop of Salisbury is recounted in my story of the Montacutes.

The legend of the White Bird was first published in a 1641 tract entitled: *A true Relation of an Apparition in the likeness of a Bird with a White Breast that appeared hovering over the Death Beds of some of the children of Mr James Oxenham of Sale Monachorum Devon, Gent.* The frontispiece of this tract in the British Library has an engraving of four compartments, each showing the White Bird hovering over the death-beds of four of the Oxenham family, their names and ages, and those of the witnesses to the apparitions. Joseph Hall, a minister of Exeter, was commanded by his bishop to give testimony 'before a Monument could be erected in the Church for the perpetual memorial of the fact, which was accordingly performed by the care and labor of Edward Marshall, Tomb-maker under St Dunstans church in the west of Fleetstreet of whom if any may doubt may receive ample satisfaction ...' The tract was published in London, and whether its story was current in Devon at the time remains a matter much disputed.

The four members of the Oxenham family in the tract engraving were John Oxenham, who died 5 September 1635; 'Thomasine, wife of James Oxenham the younger, his brother; her sister Rebecca aged eight; and Thomasine, daughter of James and Thomasine, a baby.' In addition to these four the tract mentions Grace, the grandmother of John, 'the said bird appeared over her death-bed ... in the yeare of our Redemption 1618.' Even these names and ages have been queried by various writers, but a more serious challenge to the authenticity of the Oxenham Omen came four years later when a certain James Howell published a book to a Mr E.D., *Familiar Letters*, in which he says:

> I can tell you of a strange thing I saw lately here, and I believe 'tis true. As I passed by Saint Dunstan's in Fleetstreet the last Saturday, I stepp'd into a Lapidary or Stone-cutters Shop, to treat with the Master for a Stone to be put upon my Father's Tomb, and casting my eyes up and down, I might spie a huge Marble with a large inscription upon't, which was thus to my best remembrance ... this Stone is to be sent to a Town hard by Excester, where this happen'd.

The names he gives on the inscription are John Oxenham, his sister Mary, his mother Elizabeth, and his son James 'who died a child in his cradle ...'

The church to receive this monument was obviously St Andrew, South Tawton, where the Oxenhams worshipped, but no trace of it has ever been recorded. Baring-Gould denounced it as a concocted story by an impostor. He said the monument was not only not erected but probably never existed. He said the names and dates of the Oxenhams given in the supposed inscription did not tally with any seventeenth-century records. The whole thing was a fabrication by James Howell, imprisoned in the Fleet prison for debt, trying to pay for his keep or buy his way out of prison by writing a book. Baring-Gould's conclusions were confirmed by Polwhele, the Devon historian, in his *History of Devonshire* (1793) who says: '... the prodigy of the white bird ... seems to be little known at present to the common people of S. Tawton, nor can I find anywhere a trace of the marble stone which Mr Howell saw in the lapidary's shop in London.' Nor, according to Lyson in his *Magna Britannica*, does anything appear in the parish registers of the churchyard of Zeal Monachorum. Yet the legend continued to flourish and circulate.

Equally legendary is the wedding of the rich heiress Margaret Oxenham, which is supposed to have taken place in St Andrew's church, South Tawton. This is not mentioned in the parish registers of that church. The story is that she was engaged to marry Bertram, a local landowner who unfortunately had a serious accident – a blow on the head – which sent him mad. Margaret was quite inconsolable but as time passed she began to be courted by Sir John of Roxancave whom she finally accepted. No date can be found for this tale, but it gives us the earliest mention of the White Bird. Whilst Margaret was dressing on the morning of her wedding, the White Bird came and hovered over her. Later, as she stood before the altar, her insane former fiancé Bertram rushed into the church and stabbed her to death. It is not known whether the Oxenham Omen was a tradition of the family at that time.

The actual facts about the Oxenham family have been

rather overshadowed by these legends, but the first authentic record of John Oxenham is in an eyewitness account of the voyage Sir Francis Drake made to the West Indies in 1572 to raid the rich Spanish treasure trains. John Oxenham is mentioned several times in this account, being singled out for various obviously dangerous and responsible missions. It is also claimed that he was the first Englishman to sail a boat on the Pacific. In the north chapel of South Tawton church is the effigy of John Weekes, known locally as 'Warrior Weekes', who is named in a list of 'Captaynes of the Posse Comitatus' (County Militia) as accompanying John Oxenham with Sir Frances Drake in 1572.

In the south-east corner of the Lady Chapel is the Burgoyne Memorial, a family who were clearly great friends of the Oxenhams. The slate memorial in a frame is dated 1651, ten years *after* the Oxenham Omen was published. Since generations of these families were neighbours and friends, the Oxenhams in their manor-house in Zeal Monachorum and the Burgoynes in the Great House at South Zeal, the tradition of the White Bird must surely have been known to them.

The Burgoynes were not only an ancient family but also, in the main, a distinguished one. In 1743 John Burgoyne, afterwards an English General as well as a dramatist, eloped with a daughter of the Earl of Derby, but had to sell his army commission to pay his debts and go abroad for seven years. Owing to the Earl's generosity he was later reinstated as Lieutenant-General of the Foot Guards. He then became a reckless gambler, wrote a play *The Maid of the Oaks* produced by Garrick, and fought in the American War of Independence.

It has been recorded that it was a Burgoyne heiress who brought the Great House to the Oxenhams by marriage. The date of their departure from Devon does not survive, but it was then that the Great House became the inn known today as the Oxenham Arms, it is believed it was built in the twelfth century.

In 1743 William Oxenham died and was buried in South Tawton church. All was silent until 1882 when a letter from the Revd Henry Nutcombe Oxenham revived the legend of the Oxenham Omen. His is a far more convincing account than the Tract of 1641:

> Shortly before the death of my late uncle G.M. Oxenham Esquire, of 17 Earl's Terrace, Kensington, London, who was then the head of the family this occurred. His only surviving daughter, now Mrs Thomas Peter, – and a friend of my aunt's, Miss Roberts, who happened to be staying in the house but had never heard of the family tradition, were sitting in the dining-room, immediately under his bedroom, about a week before his death, which took place on the 15th Dec. 1873, when their attention was roused by a shouting outside the window. On looking out they observed a white bird – which might have been a pigeon, – but if so, was an unusually large one, – perched on the thorntree outside the windows, and it remained there for several minutes, in spite of some workmen on the opposite side of the road throwing their hats at it in the vain effort to drive it away. Miss Roberts mentioned this to my aunt at the time, though not of course attaching any special significance to it, and my aunt ... repeated it to me soon after my uncle's death ... but Mrs Thomas Peter confirms in every particular the accuracy of this statement. Of the fact, therefore, there can be no reasonable doubt, whatever interpretation may be put upon it.

This is the last record extant of the Oxenham Omen and the appearance of the White Bird. The letter is very important for it confirms the simple truth that family traditions continue until no members are left, and even then that the legend itself does not die.

THE ROBSARTS

MURDER OR NOT?

Today, even after four centuries, the legend and possible murder of Amy Robsart, wife of Robert Dudley, Earl of

Leicester, is constantly treated by eminent writers and historians as an unsolved mystery. The news of her death on Sunday 8 September 1560, not only shocked England but half Europe. Ambassadors, dumbfounded by the sensational news, hurriedly reported it to their princes and sovereigns for Amy's husband, the rakish, dashing Robert Dudley was the leading favourite of Queen Elizabeth and rumoured to be her lover. Indeed, even before her death, when Amy was living at Cumnor Place, rumours of her increasing unhappiness at her husband's infrequent visits was the subject of much speculation amongst the ambassadors. They themselves were becoming more interested in the whisperings and rumours circulating about the queen's new favourite. The Spanish ambassador in particular was ceaseless in reporting to the Escorial.

Amy Robsart was the only legitimate daughter of Sir John Robsart. She was young, very beautiful and not without wealth when she first met Robert Dudley. Her father settled property upon her as her marriage dowry. At the same time, as part of the marriage settlement, he and Dudley's father signed a deed of settlement on Robert Dudley, granting Hemsby Manor near Yarmouth to '… my son and the Lady Amie, his wife.' The couple were married on 4 June 1550 in the royal palace of Sheen, Surrey, attended by Edward VI, who made a note of this in his diary. It must have come as a great shock to the young bride when shortly after the marriage Robert Dudley and his father, the Duke of Northumberland were imprisoned in the Tower of London in 1553 in connection with the Lady Jane Grey affair.

She was very fond of travelling about the country, and even fonder of clothes, spending much money on them. She became a close friend of the Hyde family at Denchworth, then in Berkshire but now in Oxfordshire, often visiting them there. This led to her becoming interested in nearby Cumnor, which, she was informed, she might be able to buy, certainly to rent. It had been the property of the abbots of Abingdon and was long used by them for sick monks convalescing from illness. After the death of the last Abbot Pentecost, Henry VIII granted the property to William Owen, son of George Owen physician to the king, who later rented it to Anthony Forster, Lord Dudley's steward and personal friend, who purchased the property in 1572.

Amy moved into Cumnor Place together with Mrs Pinto, her personal maid. Also living in a separate part of the mansion were Mrs Oddinsells, a widow and sister of Mr Hyde, as well as Mrs Owen, wife of William Owen, so that Amy had most friendly and pleasant company. This was soon to be badly needed as Dudley's attendances at court increased and his visits to Cumnor Place decreased. Nevertheless her letters to him were warm, revealing her deep interest in the estate. Most of these extant are in the possession of the Marquess of Bath at Longleat, Wiltshire, together with a few facsimiles in the vestry of St Michael's church, Cumnor. She wrote graciously and affectionately of 'my dear lord' when speaking of her care of the estate, the sale of sheep, wool and corn, helped by the steward Anthony Forster who was also MP for Abingdon and seemingly more interested in political business than stewardship of the estate. Her letters showed her skill in husbandry, her care of the staff, her purchase of fine dresses and of life in general. But as the months passed her husband came less often to see her and thus her knowledge of what was going on at court diminished. At first she had no suspicion whatever of what was really detaining Dudley at court but eventually she realized it was the time he spent with the queen.

Her own high rank and social position must gradually have opened her eyes to the rumours and gossip circulating in the taverns and coffee-houses of London about her handsome, finely dressed husband, skilfully dancing and intimately talking to Queen Elizabeth in what was fast becoming a love-affair. Yet Amy showed no evidence of her feelings although it was not until after her death that her personal maid, Mrs Pinto, when attending the inquest at Abingdon spoke of the sorrow and fears of her mistress, of her anxiety at the long absences. How often had she seen her mistress weeping, often 'calling on God to deliver her from her desperation.' Indeed this statement led many people to believe that she had committed suicide, rather than been killed. It is, however, hardly likely that this would have caused her to take her own life unless she were certain of her husband's infidelity. Yet there can be no doubt that those ten years of her married life at Cumnor Place must have finally convinced her of her husband's conduct. Whatever was going on in her mind came to a sudden and totally unexpected end on that fatal night Sunday 8 September 1560.

It was the night of the Abingdon Fair and Amy had given the staff permission to go and enjoy themselves there, actually urging them to go. She herself and her friends Mrs Oddinsell, and Mrs Owen would dine together and stay at home. When the staff returned late that night the house was still and quiet but they stated later that there was a strange feeling of fate or doom about it which they had never felt before. This was proved almost at once when to their horror they found the body of their mistress lying at the bottom of the wide staircase. Her neck was broken and showed unmistakeable signs of strangulation. Her face was badly bruised and her lips were blue with the poison which had been forced between them.

The most incomprehensible thing about the whole mystery of Amy Robsart's death, accident or murder, was her husband's conduct when news was brought to him of his wife's death. Dudley was at Windsor with the queen when an express messenger brought him the news. Instead of going immediately to Cumnor he ordered his cousin, Sir Thomas Blount, to make investigation and report back to him with full details. Even more incredible was his absence from her funeral. These two facts did nothing to allay the fast-growing suspicions amongst his many enemies that it was he who had ordered her to be murdered during his absence at court.

Even more suspicious was the fact that Amy Robsart's body had been secretly removed to Gloucester Hall, now Worcester College, Oxford, thence on 22 September at costly expense to St Mary's church for interment. With lavish pomp and ceremony it was attended by university and city authorities, heralds of the College of Arms and many leading court officials. The cost of all this came to some £20,000, an immense sum of money in those days.

Almost at once Amy Robsart's ghost began to haunt Cumnor Hall; servants left it empty and so it remained for another three hundred years. Her ghost moved from room to room and up and down the stairs down which, as everyone in the surrounding countryside believed, her body had been flung.

Serious attempts were made to exorcize Amy's restless and unhappy spirit to no avail, even with the customary ceremony at the time of nine clergymen attending the exorcism. The great pond Dudley had made in the garden was said to have frozen on the night of her murder though it was early in September. Cumnor Hall gradually fell into a totally abandoned ruin until 1834, when the Earl of Abingdon removed a great amount of its stonework to rebuild his mansion at Wytham. But still the truth of Amy Robsart's death was not resolved and all the concentrated efforts of Sir Thomas Blount to continue his investigations were fruitless. He found himself up against a wall of silence from the surrounding neighbourhood, particularly the gentry who obviously feared reprisals from Dudley himself.

Rumours abounded, to the joy of the insatiable Spanish ambassador: that a marriage between the Queen and

Dudley was not impossible; that Lord Burghley himself had taken the liberty of counselling the queen not to marry Dudley, risking one of her outbursts of temper or her silence. Meanwhile rumours were spreading beyond Berkshire to London and its coffee-houses and taverns where few people held any good opinion of Dudley. Other facts began to emerge about Dudley's personal friend and steward who had leased Cumnor Hall to Amy Robsart and another unknown conspirator who had seized Amy after her friends had left and all her staff gone from Cumnor on that fatal night. It was rumoured that they had tried to force poison down her throat, and failing, had strangled her and thrown her down the stairs, and that orders for her death had been given by Dudley himself so that he could marry the queen.

So convinced was Sir Thomas Blount that foul play was the reason for Amy's death that he actually consulted her own half-brother, John Appleyard who was vague about the whole matter, 'the great misfortune which had occurred in the house of Master Forster.'

Seven years later Sir Thomas Blount was summoned before the Privy Council who were debating the whole question of the circumstances of Dudley's collaboration, his absence from Cumnor Hall at the time of the tragedy and his refusal to leave Windsor at once to find out what had happened to his wife. It was at this meeting that Sir Thomas Blount was astounded to hear that John Appleyard had made yet another statement to the Privy Council when summoned, to the effect that whilst not actually accusing Dudley or implying his guilt he had said: 'While I do not hold Dudley guilty I think it would not be difficult to find out the guilty parties.' This significant statement must have seemed to Sir Thomas Blount a retraction of his earlier statement.

A trial was ordered to be held in an effort to solve this mystery. No records exist of the coroner's inquest, if indeed one was held and in fact the trial at Abingdon seems to have been something of a farce. There were no witnesses to be called because there were none at the time of Amy's death. Both Dudley and Blount bribed the jury heavily; without telling Blount, Dudley effectively silenced the foreman, getting him to give the verdict in Dudley's favour. Lady Warwick's correspondence at the time of the trial speaks tellingly of the jury, saying: 'He, Dudley, doth protest too much,' adding excerpts that prove beyond question both he and Blount were in the closest communication with the jury during the trial and after it. It was no surprise to all who sat in the court when the jury returned a verdict of not guilty declaring 'for after a most searching enquiry they could find no presumption of evil doing.'

The queen and Dudley seemed closer than ever until he endeavoured to have Black Rod dismissed from his high office. Elizabeth, always infuriated by any interference in her power over her subjects, lost her temper violently. Their delicate relationship came to a sudden end when the queen was informed of Dudley's secret marriage to Douglas, the daughter of Lord Howard of Effingham, brought to her knowledge by one of her many spies. She was beside herself with jealous fury, even threatening to send him to the Tower. The marriage was a disaster and he had by her what in his will he called 'his base son' since he was born just two days after the marriage. He never acknowledged it publicly and made many efforts to repudiate her. Some say he attempted to poison her and thus renew once more his hopes of marrying the queen.

When news of this fresh scandal reached the public through wild rumours that proved to be true circulated in ballads and lampoons, fresh evidence came to light about the death of his first wife Amy Robsart. The fresh evidence revealed that just before Amy's death messengers had been sent to Dr Bayley, a famous professor of physic at Oxford to obtain a poison for her. The doctor, however, refused to prescribe one, 'knowing her to be perfectly well at the time and that if they poisoned her under the name of his potion he might be hanged for a cover for their sin.' Yet still Dudley and the queen remained close together, incredible as it seems now.

Dudley for a third time defied the queen when, once again in secret he married Lettice Knollys, daughter of Sir Francis Knollys KG, widow of Walter Devereux, Earl of Essex, whose son Robert, 2nd Earl was later beheaded by Elizabeth. This time the queen's anger was terrifying when she was informed of the news. She commanded Dudley to appear before her at once, bitterly upbraiding him and finally giving him a stinging slap on the face and ordering him to leave her Court and threatening to send both him and that 'she-wolf his wife' to the Tower.

It was the beginning of the end of any influence he might ever have had over the queen. He failed as Governor of the Netherlands granted to him by Elizabeth and he and his wife retired to Cornbury Park in Oxfordshire, his health already worsening. There, one day whilst hunting, he came face to face with the ghost of Amy Robsart. Legend has it that she gave him a solemn warning of his imminent death and that he would soon be joining her once again. Even in recent years it is said that Amy's ghost has been seen there. Five days later he was dead, as scandalous rumours spread abroad that he had yet again obtained poison to get rid of his wife. The story was given to someone by Ben Jonson the celebrated playwright, 'that Dudley had a bottle of liquor which he had willed her in any faintness and which she had known it was poison, given him and so he died.'

His extravagant funeral cost the huge sum in those days of £40,000, double the sum he had spent on Amy Robsart's funeral. The queen, expressed her great sorrow in a very strange way. 'His death,' says Rapin, 'drew tears from the queen who nevertheless ordered his goods to be sold at private sale for payment of the sums she had lent him.'

Perhaps the saddest records of Dudley and his beautiful

first wife Amy Robsart are to be found at Cumnor in the vestry of St Michael's church. A splendid stone statue of Queen Elizabeth I, said to be have been erected by Dudley, formerly in the garden of Dean Court, is now oddly out of place in the north aisle vestry. It stands near some of the facsimile letters of both Amy Robsart to 'my dear lord' and Anthony Forster, a portrait showing how very beautiful she was, and detailed bills from her London tailor, two of which arrived after her death. In another part of the church is the stone monument of Anthony Forster, *c*.1572, believed to have been the actual murderer of Amy Robsart, carried out by Dudley's orders. Ironically they are all together in death as in life.

For very many years after Amy's death her ghost continued to haunt the house and grounds, so that local people were afraid to go near either the abandoned and ruined house or its desolate unkempt grounds. Only owls and birds lived there and always 'the flapping of the raven's wings' mentioned in a poem of the eighteenth-century poet Mickle. To the west of the church are all that is left of the broken walls and the fireplace of the once splendid hall. Grass and weeds cover the vast outlined space of the once great mansion and even today over all there is an indefinable sadness and uneasiness as if the ghost of Amy Robsart will always be there. The mystery of her tragic death is still insoluble after four centuries, but the legend remains as legends always do.

THE SHONKS

THE UNIQUE TOMB

After nine centuries the legend of the Shonks family remains an insoluble mystery in spite of considerable research made by Hertfordshire historians and various other writers and scholars. Even the family name is subject to much speculation, *viz* Shonks, Shonkes, Shank,

Knightshank, even Sank. The finally accepted version appears in the extraordinary legend which centres upon the activities of Piers Shonks. All that is historically true is that he held the lordship of a manor in Brent Pelham, was of Norman origin, died in 1086 and was a great huntsman. It is said that he was a giant and slew a dragon, this establishing him later as the Hertfordshire St George. All that remains today is his remarkable tomb in Brent Pelham church, and the nearby moat that once surrounded his manor-house. Behind these few facts lie only traditions and legends, all different. The main legend concerns the slaying of a dragon by Piers Shonks.

A dragon was also called a serpent, a worm, or, most terrifying of all, a wyvern – a combination of them all in a monster with wings, huge strong claws and a snake-like body, which breathed fire. It ravaged the countryside, eating cattle and children. The tale of Piers Shonks concerns such a monster which used to lurk deep down under the roots of a giant yew-tree standing in a meadow between the fields named Great and Little Pepsells in Brent Pelham. Such was the havoc caused by this formidable beast that the great huntsman Piers Shonks made up his mind to kill it and set out one day with his hounds. His hounds were said to have been the fastest in the district, so fast that they were believed to have had wings. The dogs began digging at the roots of the yew-tree until the dragon emerged; and then a terrible battle began between Shonks and the monster, ending in its death when Shonks rammed his spear down its throat. Its writhing death struggle had scarcely ceased when the Evil One, the Devil, appeared before Shonks, threatening that he would have his revenge on Shonks after his death by claiming both his body and his soul whether he were to be buried within or outside the church.

Fear of the Devil was great in those times, perhaps even more than of dragons, and Shonks took great notice of this threat. On his deathbed he asked for his bow and arrow to be brought to him and he gave instructions that he was to be interred wherever the arrow should fall. Such commands were given by a similar folk hero (for that was what Shonks was to become) when the outlaw Robin Hood fired his last arrow. Shonks swore open defiance to the Devil's threat by telling him that his soul belonged to heaven but his body should rest neither in nor out of church but beyond the Devil's reach. He then shot his arrow which passed through the church window, through the chancel and fell at the north wall. There, within the fabric of the wall and neither in nor out of the church, his body was interred and his tomb placed.

The tomb of O Piers Shonks, as it was called, is as eccentric, legendary and enigmatic as the man himself. In a deep recess within the north wall of Brent Pelham church a black Petworth marble slab covering the tomb may be seen today. Above it on a wooden board is a Latin inscription which has been translated (obviously by a much later vicar) as:

> Nothing of Cadmus nor St George, those names,
> Of great renown, survives them but their fames;
> Time was so sharp set as to make no Bones
> Of theirs, nor of their monumental stones.
> But Shonks one serpent kills, t'other defies,
> And in this wall as in a fortress lies.

It is headed by the words:

> O PIERS SHONKS
> WHO DIED ANNO 1086.

Cadmus was a local giant who had fought a great battle with Shonks, another giant.

The much later explanation of another part of the Shonks legend came from the fact that when the tomb was opened in 1836 by two churchwardens, probably for examination of the stonework, extraordinarily large bones were discovered. Mrs Hudson, a parishioner of Barkway, said that Mr Morris, probably one of the churchwardens and another man, 'each took a bone out of the tomb. One joint was as long as an ordinary man's finger but it was double-jointed. Mr Morris never had any peace with this bone and had to put it back in the tomb.' The other man suffered but not to the same extent, 'but he never knew the going of the bone or when it disappeared'.

Further evidence that people were convinced that Shonks was a giant is given by Nathaniel Simon, the county historian in his *History of Hertfordshire* (1728) when he says:

> ... the Relation given me by an old Farmer in the Parish, who valued himself for being born in the Air that Shonk breathed. He saith that Shonk was a Giant that dwelt in this Parish, who fought with giant of *Barkway*, named Cadmus, and worsted him; upon which *Barkway* hath paid a Quit-Rent to *Pelham* ever since.

IN C.P.C. Barclay's book *The Story of Brent Pelham*, he states that in 1865 the owner of Beeches Manor, a fine sixteenth-century mansion, was a great eccentric who lived there with all his horses, pigs and cattle and 'four strapping wenches who had nothing to do but obey their master and play cards with him'. He had been appointed the man to collect the Dragon money which was paid annually by the village of Barkway in gratitude to Shonks for killing their dragon. Barclay starts his book with a most interesting statement: 'The earliest known inhabitant of Brent Pelham is also perhaps the most notable in its history.' He then gives the legend of Piers Shonks and the killing of the dragon.

Nathaniel Salmon also tells us in his *History of Hertfordshire* that a certain Simon de Furneuse gave his name to Furneux Pelham adjacent to the other two villages, Brent Pelham and Stocking Pelham, the surname

Pelham coming from Walter de Pelham who was granted land and the lordship of Pelham during the reign of Edward I. Simon de Furneuse seems also to have had land granted to him by the same king and must also have been an overlord. Nathaniel Salmon states that this Simon de Furneuse imposed a fine of 40*s*. 6*d*. as an annual Quit-Rent to one Gilbert Sank for 'failure to pay his homage and services'. Salmon then goes on to say: 'Sank and Shonk are so near, especially if we suppose the copier to be a Norman, that I may be indulged to believe that they are the same name.' Such an unprovable assertion has caused still more consternation in the legend of Piers Shonks.

That Shonks did live nearby is obviously true since Brent Pelham was a tiny village before it was burnt down. A full and detailed account of the original site is given by R.T. Andrews in his book *Moats and Moated Sites of Hertfordshire*. After the fire that badly destroyed the village of Brent Pelham during the reign of Henry I (1154–89) only moats and mounds marked the reputed sites of destroyed houses. The site of Shonks manor, according to R.T. Andrews, was enclosed within four-and-a-quarter acres and was a moated dwelling. It was known to Salmon in 1728 as Shonks Barn, but almost a century before when visited by Cole it was known as Shonks Garden or Shonks Moat, and is called so even today because of its moat. It is the indeterminable mixture of fancy and history, an integral part of all legends, that makes it so interesting that giants, dragons, and fairies are believed in by many ancient families.

To retun to Shonks' tomb, G.W. Gerish, in his fascinating book *A Tour through Hertfordshire*, has a scholarly chapter headed *The Story of O Piers and the Pelham Dragon* (1921). He states that Shonks not only gave instructions about where his body should be interred but also directed that a representation of his achievements should be made upon his tomb. These elaborately carved figures have continued to puzzle scholars and writers alike.

The Evangelists are represented by four symbols, Angel,

Lion, Eagle and Bull. The Angel is depicted as bearing the soul of the deceased to Heaven, represented in the usual medieval manner of a naked man with his hands folded in prayer, wrapped in a winding-sheet. In the centre is a cross, the stem of which is the stem of Piers Shonks' spear thrust into the jaws of what is more a serpent than a dragon, coiled at the foot of the slab. There are also the figures of the hounds who helped Shonks to locate and fight the dragon. Ecclesiologists recognize these carvings as emblematical of the triumph of Christianity over paganism.

It is interesting to read what the authoritative *Victoria County History of Hertfordshire* has to say about the tomb.

> ... the tomb in the church which an 18th-century inscription ascribes to O Piers Shonks, who died in 1086. But the tomb dates only from the late 13th century. The name Shonks has been more plausibly derived from the early tenancy of Gilbert Sanke ... or others of his family, of whom may have been Matthew Shanke and William Shanke of Pelham, who occur in 1324 and 1353 respectively, and Peter Shank, who later in the century was lessee of the manor of Barwick in Barkway.

It seems incredible that this Peter, or indeed a Peter Knightshank who lived in Barkway during the same period, actually fought and killed a dragon three centuries later than Piers Shonks. Even if the most credulous person accepted the existence of dragons, or similar monsters, in the eleventh century, there seems to be no evidence that dragons were ravaging the English countryside in the fourteenth century.

All is wide open to conjecture, to scholarly research, to belief in legends or fabulous beasts and giants, for the legend of O Piers Shonks, 'the last dragon slayer' remains an insoluble mystery. Is it any wonder, therefore, that he has gone down in history and legend as 'The Hertfordshire St George'?

THE FAMILIES OF WILLIAM THE CONQUEROR AND TYRELL

RED RUFUS

In 1087 William the Conqueror, illegitimate son of Robert the Magnificent, Duke of Normandy, and a tanner's daughter, died at the age of sixty. William of Malmesbury, the twelfth-century chronicler records that 'in his youth he was so observant of his chastity that people thought him impotent.' After giving Matilda twelve children he seems to have proved his virility, the chronicler praising him for his fidelity and tenderest affection towards his wife. He left eight daughters and three sons, Robert, William and Henry. Contrary to common practice, the second son William Rufus then became king of England. He reigned for thirteen years as one of the very worst of the medieval kings.

His death, by accident or murder, in the New Forest in 1100, became not only a completely unsolved mystery but also one of the greatest legends preserved in the folklore of Hampshire and England. The new king was as fat as his father, red-faced or red-headed (hence his nickname 'Rufus'), vicious, cruel, as hard a man as his father, avaricious and explosively blasphemous. He ruthlessly punished the Church by exiling Anselm, Archbishop of Canterbury, confiscating the revenues, and leaving the bishoprics of a great number of the richest sees vacant. He was hated by the church and the barons since he imposed heavy feudal fines on them. His elder brother Robert, easy-going, good-natured, bitterly disappointed at being only Duke of Normandy instead of King of England went on the first crusade, pawning his estates to Rufus. Their younger brother Henry, later Henry I, only inherited silver.

The legend began the night before the death of Rufus on 2 August 1100. Rufus was at Castle Malwood to enjoy a day of hunting in the New Forest, a pastime also enjoyed by his father. William of Malmesbury recorded an unusual story he heard from the exiled Anselm of France in a conversation with Hugh, the abbot of Glugny, both men of truth. The conversation between them naturally turned on William Rufus who had caused such harm to Anselm. Hugh told him, 'Last night the king was brought before God; and by a deliberate judgment incurred the sorrowful sentence of damnation.' These prophetic words remained forever in the minds of the hearers long after the king's sudden death.

The king himself had a terrible dream that night. He dreamt that he was let blood by a surgeon and that the stream of blood, reaching to heaven, clouded the light and interrupted the day, forcing this blasphemer to cry to St Mary for protection. The terrified king then awoke, shouted for light to be brought and commanded his attendants not to leave him for a single moment. They stayed with him until daybreak.

The day had scarcely begun when Richard Fitz Hamon, one of the nobility, came to Rufus to tell him that a monk had told him of a fearful dream he had had last night which seemed to be a premonition of the king's imminent death, but William laughed it away with the words 'He is a monk and dreams for money like a monk,' and he handed Fitz Hamon one hundred shillings to give the dreamer. Nevertheless the king was greatly disturbed and decided to forego the dawn hunt.

The New Forest itself had already had two tragedies, one a Richard, bastard son of William I, the other, another Richard, bastard son of Rufus's brother Robert. A third tragedy was imminent that very day, the third in the family of William the Conqueror. Rufus's agitated mind sought solace in excessive amounts of alcohol even before he was served with dinner, a meal shared by Sir Walter Tyrell, a Norman baron of Poix and Pontoise, who had just returned from Normandy at the invitation of the king. He had arrived the day before. Rufus had sent for the huntsman and ordered him to bring six new arrows saying that the hunt would start in the early evening. He then gave Sir Walter Tyrell two of them, with the words: 'The best arrows to the best shot.' He could not even imagine what was to happen.

The Royal Hunt took place in the New Forest. The hunting party, which included Rufus's brother Henry was directed by the huntsman to various positions in the forest glades to which the beaters would drive the stags. Rufus and Tyrell were together, Rufus of course would let loose the first arrow. What happened next was total confusion and, even today, historians and writers have found no solution to what has been described as the tragedy of the New Forest.

Rufus and Tyrell were standing near Stony Cross when a stag bounded into the glade. The king immediately drew his bow, let fly the arrow which wounded the stag, and sheltering his eyes with his hand from the powerful westering sun he watched the animal pass out of sight. Since William of Malmesbury's account of what happened is the earliest, and since he was himself an abbot whose word would never be challenged, he writes:

> At that instant Walter, conceiving a noble exploit, which was while the king's attention was otherwise occupied, to transfix another stag which by chance came near him, unknowing and without power to prevent it, Oh, gracious God!, pierced his breast with a fatal arrow. On receiving the wound, the king uttered not a word; but breaking off the shaft of the weapon where it projected from his body, fell upon the wound, by which he accelerated his death. Walter immediately ran up, but he found him senseless, and speechless he leaped swiftly upon his horse, and escaped …

This simple account, written thirty-two years after the king's death, should perhaps need no further additions; yet from then onwards speculation began, narrator after narrator adding to previous speculations until one is today quite bewildered by it all. Why did Tyrell act so swiftly, was it fear, shock? He was the only one near the king and would therefore be considered a murderer, for none of the party would believe his denial of what really happened.

Some historians and writers have even gone to the length of reconstructing the actual method of his death, the most modern being that it was not an accident, but murder. This is because whoever fired the fatal arrow was at least eighty yards away from the king and protected by trees, thus Tyrell was placed at an impossible angle. If the arrow had glanced off the stag, as other writers say, its force would have been expended and it would have dropped to the ground. The shot must have been a direct one and in front of Rufus since it went straight into his breast, so it is possible that the huntsman himself might have shot the fatal arrow. If it were the huntsman, then there might have been the more serious regicide plot on hand. The strongest evidence in support of this point of view is the fact that the king's brother Henry, having been told the news, acted with astonishing dispatch, similar to his brother's alacrity in being crowned after his father's death.

Henry first heard of the news by chance. He was in another part of the forest when his bow-string broke and he called at a cottage belonging to a forester, to be greeted by a woman who curtseyed to him and greeted him as the king. He mounted his horse and galloped as hard as he could to Winchester to seize the royal treasure; in spite of the fact that De Breteuil, also in the hunting party, pointed out that Henry's brother Robert, who was on the first crusade, was rightful heir to the throne. Within six days, the usurper Henry was crowned King of England on 6 August 1100. Rufus had died at 7 p.m. on that fatal Thursday. About two hours later the body was found by a charcoal burner who loaded it on to his cart and set out for Winchester, some twenty miles away. Malmesbury tells us it went '... with blood dripping all the way. Here it was committed to the ground within the tower, attended by many of the nobility, though lamented by few.'

It was not only the nobility, however, who did not lament Rufus's death. The clergy were united in proclaiming that this was God's judgment on a man who defied and denied them. They had no pity for a king who had deprived Anselm of his office and sent him into exile, and emptied the abbeys by withholding appointments and confiscating the revenues. Such conduct deserved divine punishment. Rufus himself was refused a conditional absolution by the Church as their final condemnation of his life.

Rufus himself had had more than uneasy premonitions both the night before and on the day of his death. He may also have remembered the pagan belief in the divine victim, the king who was also a god, who when called upon was expected to give his life and his blood to rejuvenate the earth. Several writers have suggested this role for Rufus. The date of his death was also significant for it was the day after Lugnasad, the Celtic harvest festival, a traditional day of sacrifice. On the previous May Day eve, the Celtic festival of spring, William's illegitimate son had died, also in a hunting accident. Some writers felt that the boy had tried to offer himself in his father's place though it was the life of the king himself that was the tradition.

The key figure in this high drama of death in the New Forest was Sir Walter Tyrell. Did he murder the king? Was he part of a plot of regicide? Did he aid and abet the huntsman? The king had many enemies apart from his own brothers, they included the powerful family of the Clares. Tyrell's wife Alice was a Clare, king of the powerful overlords who were close friends of Rufus' brother the new king Henry. It has been said by some writers that the most damning evidence against Tyrell was given by the huntsman who said that the arrow which caused the king's death was one of the two the king had given him that day saying 'The best arrows to the best shot.'

Abbot Suger of St Denis in his *Life of King Louis VI of France*, written forty-four years after Rufus' death, says that he often heard Tyrell actually deny that he was with the king in that part of the wood that day, or saw him at all during the hunt. Yet Malmesbury asserts that he was alone with the king.

Even on his death-bed Tyrell was said to have repeated his denial that he was the murderer of the king. So who was? Charles II had the memorial stone marking the spot where Rufus died railed off, but it has long disappeared. The famous Rufus Stone near Minstead was erected in 1745 and still exists and is seen by thousands of people each year visiting the New Forest, but the mystery of who killed the king remains unsolved.

Twenty-one years after the death of Rufus, *The Anglo-Saxon Chronicle* wrote his bitter epitaph: 'The king was killed with an arrow while hunting by one of his men ... He was hated by almost all his people and abhorrent to God. This his end testified, for he died in the midst of his sins, without repentance, or any atonement for his evil deeds.'

It is incredible to think a second member of the Tyrell family should be involved in another royal drama as insoluble as the regicide in the New Forest. According to *Burke's Extinct and Dormant Baronetcies*:

> The family of Tirrell is one of great note and antiquity and for more than six hundred years its chief, in a direct line enjoyed the honour of knighthood. Sir Walter Tirrell, held at the general survey, from the Conqueror, the lordship of Langham, in Essex. This is the knight to whom, whether truly or falsely, the death of William *Rufus*, has been attributed by our historians.

During these six centuries various members of the family held high honour in Essex and elsewhere, increased still more by marriages into other families, but seem to have lived consistently in Essex and still do so. Sir John Tyrell, as the name is now spelt, was appointed carpenter at the new works at Calais by Henry III. He fought at Agincourt in 1415 and was Speaker of the House of Commons. In the church of All Saints, East Horndon, Essex, there was a remarkable incised stone effigy of his wife Alice, as well as a number of other monuments, damaged and defaced to such an extent now by vandalism that the church has become redundant. An All Saints membership has been formed by the families of Tyrell to protect what remains, there being a considerable number of them in the United States of America.

The most remarkable member of the Tyrell family was Sir James. He was a Yorkist during the bloody Wars of the Roses, and for his services was appointed Master of the Horse to Richard III. Henry VII later appointed him Governor of Guisnes but had him executed in 1502. This might well have been because, like so many others he had defected from the Yorkist to the Lancastrian cause. His most significant place in history is unhappily linked with regicide, following that of the head of the line Sir Walter Tyrell. He was commanded by Richard III to murder his two nephews, then in the Tower. He did not commit the murder himself, but suborned two hit men, Deighton and Forrest to do so. This was another insoluble mystery in the family history, for the bodies of the two remained undiscovered until 1674; the skeletons were buried in Westminster Abbey. Shakespeare, in Richard III, act IV, scene III, describes King Richard asking, 'Kind Tyrell, am I happy in thy news?,' to be assured that the children had been smothered.

Historians are still confused and divided about this murder as also the New Forest murder, but the fact remains that the name of Tyrell is still prominent in Hampshire, notably Tyrell's ford and Tyrell's forge, where the blacksmith reversed his horse's shoes to deceive any pursuer of Tyrell. For a long period afterwards the blacksmith paid a yearly fine to the Crown in expiation of his crime.

3 *Ceremonies, Privileges and Traditions*

THE CONYERS AND POLLARDS

THE FALCHION

Unbelievable as it may seem the celebrated legend of the Lambton Worm, (described on page 151 in this book) is very similar to that of the Conyers family of Sockburn, also in the County Palatinate of Durham. Their story was also first narrated by Robert Surtees, historian and antiquarian. The Conyers legend is perhaps even more interesting because it involves a very remarkable family tradition which began in the reign of Richard I and continued periodically until the early nineteenth century. The head of the line was Roger, appointed by William the Conqueror as 'Constable of Durham Castle and Keeper of all the arms of ye souldiers within the Castle … to him and his heires mailes for ever …'

Members of this Norman family were also Lords of Bishopton, Durham, and granted the manor of Sockburn. They showed their strength by building a peel-house as defence against the Border invaders. Roger left a grandson, also named Roger who seems to have alienated the direct line for it passed to Gilfrid whose younger son was Sir John Conyers. The male line continued into Charles I's reign when it became extinct. The female line continued through marriages to Talbot, the Earls of Shrewsbury and the Stonor family in Oxfordshire. Sir John

Conyers was certainly lord of the manor of Sockburn in 1334. He died in 1396. It was from this manor and this man that first the legend and then the ceremony began, faithfully recorded by Robert Surtees' in 1823. He deals with the legend first and quotes as follows,

> In an ould Manuscript wh I have sene of ye descent of Conyers, there is writ as followeth: Sr John Conyers, Knt. slew yt monstrous and poysonous vermine or wyverne, and aske o werme, wh overthrew and devoured many people in fight, for that ye sent of yt poison was so strong yt no person might abyde it. And by ye providence of Almighty God this John Conyers, Kt overthrew ye saide monster, and slew it. But before he made this enterprise, having but one sonne, he went to the Church of Sockburne in compleate armour, and offered up yt his onely sonne to ye Holy Ghost. Yt place where this great serpent laye was called Graystane; and as it is written in ye same manuscript, this John lieth buried in Sockburne Church in compleat armour before the Conquest.

The last three words are not easily understood since Sir John died during the reign of Richard Coeur de Lion; the date 1396 was given at his inquest. The place where the monster was slain is still pointed out to people in a field next to the church. Not only was Sir John buried in complete armour but there is carved on his tomb, and at his feet, a dog and a monstrous coiled serpent, giving proof to posterity of what he had accomplished. Robert Surtees adds his own convictions in his manuscript when he says: '... proves that the legend is of no modern origin, and I will not doubt that some gallant exploit is veiled under this chivalrous tale, with at least an adumbration of truth.' He states that in 1789 there was a painted window in the church showing the weapon with which Sir John slew the monster. This was a falchion, known as the Sockburn Faulchion and it originated from a feudal service paid by the lord of the manor of Sockburn to the Bishop of Durham.

The falchion was a short-bladed, sickle-shaped sword. One side of the pommel bore the arms of England, the other the eagle as borne by Morcar, the Saxon Earl of Northumberland. The ceremony took place on the Bishop's first entry into his diocese in the County Palatinate when the falchion was handed to him by the Lord of Sockburn or his steward. Robert Surtees gives the following description of the ceremony:

> At the first entrance of the Bishop into his Diocese, the Lord of Sockburn, or his Steward, meets him in the middle of the river Tees, at Nesham-ford, or on Croft-bridge, and presents a faulchion to the Bishop with these words: 'My Lord Bishop, I here present you with the faulchion wherewith the champion Conyers slew the worm, dragon, or fiery flying serpent, which destroyed man, woman, and child; in memory of which, the King then reigning gave him the manor of Sockburn, to hold by this tenure, that upon the first entrance of every Bishop into the country, this faulchion should be presented.' The Bishop takes the faulchion in his hand, and immediately returns it courteously to the person who presents it, wishing the Lord of Sockburn health and a long enjoyment of the manor.

This curious feudal ceremony continued until 1826 when Sir Edward Blackett owned Sockburn Manor. The Sockburn Falchion is now in Durham Cathedral where it may be seen in the Durham Cathedral treasury.

Strange as it may seem there is an identical ceremony concerning the presentation of a falchion by another family in the Palatinate of Durham at Bishop Auckland, some eleven miles away. It may well be earlier than that held by the Conyers family, for the first mention of the Pollards occurs in the Domesday Book. In the eleventh year of Bishop Skirlaw it was recorded that Dionescia Pollard had died, seized of a parcel of land called Westland held of the bishop in socage. This was the word used at that time for the feudal tenure of land involving payment of rent or other services to a superior. In this case it was the possession of a falchion proudly and jealously held as a tradition and privilege of a great family. It was given as a reward for the first Pollard ancestor who had killed a monster called the Pollard Worm giving the right of every successive heir to their estates to assert that right to any bishop entering their lands for the first time. That ancestor became known as the champion knight Pollard of Pollard Hall. No record exists of the origin of this feudal tenure, but there is no doubt at all that the family was an illustrious and wealthy one.

As further evidence of their wealth, in addition to the Westfield property the Pollards also had a parcel of land in Hekes near to Auckland Park, another parcel of land in a place called the Halgh, held in socage of the Earl of Westmorland. They also had fifty acres in Coundon Moor. The local historian William Hutchinson tells us in his book *The history and antiquities of the county palatinate of Durham 1794* that '… the last of this family named in the records in the fifteenth year of Queen Elizabeth' (which would be 1573). It would seem, therefore, that the actual falchion was used and remains untraced, unlike the one used by the Conyers family and now in Durham Cathedral. Thereafter if there were no Pollard heirs it must have been that successive lords of the manor of one or other of the former Pollard possessions continued the ceremony by a speech. The words of this speech are recorded as follows:

> My Lord, I, in behalf of myself, as well as several others, possessors of the Pollard's lands, do humbly present your lordship with this falchion at your first coming here, wherewith, as the tradition goeth, he slew of old a venomous serpent, which did much harm to man and beast; and by performing this service we hold our lands.

In the book *Notes on the folklore of the northern counties of England* it is stated that this venomous serpent was also known as the Pollard Worm or the Pollard wild boar, or the Pollard brawn which, in fact, meant a dragon.

THE DYMOKES

THE KING'S CHAMPION

The high, ancient and chivalric office of Champion of England, has been proudly held for centuries by the Dymoke family of Scrivelsby Court, four miles from the Lincolnshire market-town of Horncastle. Some three or four hundred yards from their beautiful home is the church, filled with family monuments, tombs and brasses of champions to Richard III, Henry VII, Henry VIII, Charles I and the first three Georges.

This high office was supposedly founded by Duke William of Normandy when he became King of England in 1066. It was one of the king's early appointments, given to Robert Marmion, Lord of Fontenay in Normandy who fought under him. It was the first time a king had created the duty of champion. His office was 'to ride completely armed upon a barbed horse into Westminster Hall after the coronation and there to challenge to combat with whomsoever should deny the king's right to the crown.' The large effigy of a knight in chain armour in Scrivelsby church is said to be that of the great feudal Baron Philip Marmion. He died in 1292, leaving no male issue but four daughters so that the title fell into abeyance.

In 1350 his great-granddaughter Margaret de Ludlow married Sir John Dymoke bringing to him, as her dowry, not only the ancient baronial estate of Scrivelsby, but the hereditary title of Champion of England. His right to this was immediately challenged by a kinsman but was overruled by the Court of Claims, thus enabling Sir John to act as champion for the first time at the coronation of Richard II (1377). The title has been held by the family ever since, except during the Wars of the Roses. Sir Thomas

Dymoke, who was champion to the Yorkist Edward IV, went over to the Lancastrian cause under the Earl of Warwick, for which treachery he was taken prisoner, attainted of his honours and beheaded. The king, however, restored all honours and titles to his son Sir Robert Dymoke. As so often happened to great families in those uncertain times, the Dymokes, facing ruin, dishonour and even extinction, had the good fortune to survive.

They were staunch Catholics and like so many other families were prepared to die for their faith during the persecutions by Elizabeth I. Sir Robert Dymoke, in spite of being in a weak state of health, was actually dragged before the Bishop of Lincoln for examination, imprisoned in the city of Lincoln for heresy and, dying there, was buried in Scrivelsby church.

The feudal grandeur, colour and splendour of the last ceremony in which the Champion of England carried out his duties was traditional pageantry at its best. After the coronation of George IV in Westminster Abbey the procession moved to Westminster Hall. The king took his seat at a sumptuous banquet among the nobility of the land. After the giving and receiving of gifts the first course was removed from the laden tables. Suddenly the magnificent hall with its great double hammer-beam roof resounded with a fanfare from the royal trumpeters in the gallery above the triumphal arch through which the Champion of England rode into the great hall.

He was seated on a richly caparisoned piebald horse, completely clad in glittering armour, a great panache of plumes upon his helm, a mail gauntlet held high up in his right hand. He and his personal page were outflanked by his two esquires and their pages in half-armour to left and right. One page carried the champion's lance, the other his targe or shield, on which were emblazoned the Dymoke arms. On the full achievement of their coat of arms was their motto, 'Pro Rege Dimico' ('I fight for the king'), a proud and clever combination of a play on their surname and office.

The champion in clear ringing tones then issued his challenge.

> If any person of what degree soever, high or low, shall deny or gainsay our Sovereign Lord King he, the last being deceased, to be the right heir to the Imperial Crown of this Kingdom, or that he ought not to enjoy the same, here is his Champion who saith he lieth and that he is a false traitor, being ready in person to combat with him and in this quarrel will adventure his life against him on whatsoever day shall be appointed.

After pausing a few moments, the champion, in support of his challenge, threw his gauntlet clattering to the ground.

Amidst shouts of 'Long Live the King' from the whole assembly, the herald picked up the gauntlet and returned it to the champion, who with his cavalcade then moved halfway into the hall and repeated the challenge. The third time he rode to the foot of the throne. The herald read the challenge at the foot of the steps, and the champion flung the gauntlet defiantly down for the last time. No acceptance of the challenge has ever been recorded.

The royal cupbearer then handed the king a gold cup full of wine, from which he drank to his champion, who himself drinking and crying out 'Long live the King,' handed the cup to his page to bear it away for him, as the traditional privilege and honour. In safer times the number of gold cups collected by the Dymoke family were kept in their home but this is no longer possible, a bitter reflection of life today.

It is sad that this unique ceremony was last carried out at the accession of George IV to the throne. No reason has been given but it might well have been thought that the calibre of such a king was not worth a challenge. This last ceremony was, possibly, the greatest one of all. A full report by an eyewitness was fortunately written in the

Gentleman's Magazine of 1821, the year of the coronation. The champion on this occasion was escorted by two of the foremost figures of that time, on his right by the Duke of Wellington and on his left by Lord Howard of Effingham, both magnificently dressed in scarlet and ermine robes, wearing their own coronets, and carrying their staves of office. 'A Mahomedan Paradise' wrote another eyewitness of the huge assembly of peeresses in their robes and coronets. The Privy Councillors wore clothes of white and blue satin, with trunk hose as in the time of Elizabeth I. The pages wore coats of scarlet with gold lace, white silk hose and white rosettes.

Immediately after the champion had ridden his cavalcade from the ceremony, his page bearing the traditional gold cup, Garter King of Arms, surrounded by all his officers, read the Proclamation from the steps of the throne in Latin, French and English, repeating it twice more whilst walking in the reverse order of the champion's entry. At the entrance of the hall all the heralds cried out 'Largesse', a medieval privilege at tournaments when it was their custom to ask for gifts of money for their services.

Though the ceremony is no longer enacted, the Dymokes still carry out their duty at each coronation of our sovereigns, which has continued through the centuries. As Honourable the Sovereign's Champion and Standard Bearer of England they officiated at the Coronation of Edward VII, George V and George VI. Their most recent duty was carried out for the coronation of Elizabeth II in 1953. Thus for nine centuries their proud title has remained unique in the history of British chivalry, heraldry and tradition.

THE FAMILY OF JOHN OF GAUNT

THE HOCKTIDE CEREMONY

When on 10 April 1362 the Duchess Maud of Bavaria died, all her considerable estate in Hungerford, Berkshire, passed to her younger sister Blanche, who was the wife of John of Gaunt, fourth son of Edward III, created Duke of Lancaster and Earl of Leicester in right of his wife. It was a significant event in the history of the town. Not only did it pass into the Duchy of Lancaster but the tradition is that it was given a much prized Royal Charter from Edward III. Full manorial and fishing-rights were given to them by John of Gaunt and a personal present from him of the celebrated horn, a cherished treasure.

Long-standing and tenaciously held traditions arose from all these gifts, notably the celebrated Hocktide Court and its Jury. On the Tuesday after Easter week down to the present day, thousands of visitors pour into the town to witness it. It is a festival and ceremonial unique in England. The original, ancient and much-battered brass horn, its rim surmounted by the family badge of a crescent encircling an estoile (a five-pointed star), is not used for the opening ceremony, instead one substituted in the reign of Charles I and inscribed with the words 'JOHN A GAUN DID GIVE AND GRANT THE RIALL FISHING TO HUNGERFORD TOWN FROM ELDREN STUB TO IRISH STIL EXEPING SOME SEVERAL MIPOUND' is used. In accordance with ancient customs such a gift would have been a guarantee of rights. It has, however, always been maintained that there were two copies of a written charter, one of which was burnt when John of Gaunt's Savoy Palace in London was destroyed by fire. The other was stolen from Hungerford during the reign of Elizabeth I.

There is no record at all of how long John of Gaunt stayed in the manor or the town, but his first wife Blanche of Lancaster gave him a son later Henry IV, and two daughters. His second marriage was with Constance of

Castile and Leon, through which he became King of Castile. His third marriage was with Katherine Swynford.

Edward III kept a very tight rein on his son so that he possessed limited powers over the Duchy estates. In Hungerford itself the king refused to allow him to reassert the full manorial rights formerly exercised by the Earls of Leicester. John of Gaunt's young nephew Richard II altered all that drastically, allowing him to exercise sovereign rights not only over Eddington Manor but over all the estate of the Duchy of Lancaster.

According to the Royal lineage in Burke's Peerage:

> The Duke (John of Gaunt) m. 3rdly, 1396–7 Katherine, formerly his mistress, widow of Sir Hugh Swynford, Kt. and dau. and co-heir of Sir Payn Roet, Kt., of Hainault, Guinne King-of-Arms ... having by her had issue, surnamed Beaufort, born in adultery, who were legitimated by Statute 20 Rec II (1397), but were not thereby enabled to inherit the Crown.

An illegitimate great-great-grandson of John of Gaunt was created Earl of Worcester in 1513/4 and is the line of the present Duke of Beaufort, whose home is Badminton House where the annual horse trials are held. It is not open to the public.

The memory of John of Gaunt in Hungerford is renewed annually by the Hocktide Festival attended by thousands of visitors. To see the whole and quaint ceremony it is essential to arrive in the town early on the Tuesday following Easter week, from the moment the Constable calls his Hocktide Court and jury to attend. A replica of the precious horn John of Gaunt gave as his personal seal of the fishing rights to the town, known as the Lucas horn, is now used by the Constable.

The 'tuttimen' carry long poles decked with flowers, on the tip of which is an orange. This is exchanged for kisses from the ladies of houses which they have visited. The poles represent the medieval surveyor's staff – today's theodolite.

The immortal memory of John of Gaunt is toasted from a bowl of Plantagenet punch when the newly-elected constable and his twelve burgesses sit down to a splendid meal.

Another great tradition of which Hungerford is so proud is that of the ceremony of the presentation of the Lancastrian Red Rose to the sovereign whenever the town is honoured with a royal visit. As direct descendants of John of Gaunt, it was, during his lifetime, a tribute to his father Edward III as holder of the Duchy of Lancaster, homage to the sovereign. Three times this century has the presentation taken place before thousands of people gathered to see a great medieval custom. The first marked the coming of King George V and Queen Mary, *en route* for a private visit with friends, on 12 October 1912. The second was King George VI and Queen Elizabeth, (now the Queen Mother) on 12 March 1948. The third was the present Queen Elizabeth II, with the Duke of Edinburgh and Princess Margaret, again *en route* for another destination, on 23 April 1952.

The Red Rose is always presented to the sovereign by the Constable, accompanied by the town clerk, the town trustees and the town crier in grey uniform with scarlet facings, polished top hat and carrying his staff of office. It is a great day for the constable, who is elected annually by the tenants of ninety-nine houses holding the Kennet fishing-rights granted by John of Gaunt. It is he alone who has the honour of handing the sovereign the Lancastrian Red Rose resting on a silver salver on behalf of the citizens of Hungerford, with a brief explanation of the tradition to a new sovereign on a first visit.

This last ceremony took place before the Bear Hotel, where William of Orange once met the King's commissioners a few days before James II fled to France.

THE KNOLLYS FAMILY

THE RED ROSE

The distinguished and ancient family of Knollys, extant after six hundred years, has a rare tradition and legend, revived annually (except for one break) from 1381. It is one of the many superb London ceremonies and probably the most beautiful, the Presentation of the Knollys Rose to the Lord Mayor of London and is held in the Mansion House as near as possible to Midsummer Day. This was the fulfilment of an obligation made by Sir Robert Knollys for his heirs and assigns forever, after illegally building a footbridge across Seething Lane in the City of London.

Sir Robert Knollys was a remarkable figure who, according to *Burke's Peerage,* 'from humble fortunes attained great wealth and high reputation.' His origins are unclear but it is probable that he was a Cheshire man, and perhaps related to another Cheshire and Yorkshire family, the Calverleys. There is evidence in Froissart's *Chronicles* that they fought together in the French wars from which Sir Robert emerged as one of the outstanding soldiers of the campaign.

It was quite early on in his military career that Sir Robert distinguished himself as a leader of mercenaries against the French. It was stated in the county history of Cheshire that he could drive the enemy before him like flocks of sheep and batter down their citadels into such spiry and forked points that they went by the name of Knolles mitres. His wife Constance proved as belligerent as her husband, for in 1360 she sailed to support him in Brittany with twenty men at arms and forty archers on horseback in three ships at her own expense.

His campaigns were many, various and mostly victorious. He held a separate command with the forces sent out from England under command of John of Gaunt, Duke of Lancaster. He was chosen by the Black Prince to accompany him to Spain. He was, however, a man of many parts, who could combine cruelty and ruthlessness with great mercy all in one day. In revenge for his soldiers being beheaded by the French he ordered four of his French prisoners to be executed. In order to see that the sentence was carried out he had a scaffold for the gallows placed before the castle so that he could watch the execution. On the same day he released one or more of his captives as an act of mercy. He reached the zenith of his military career when he was summoned urgently back to England to deal with the Peasants' Revolt against Richard II, led by Jack Straw and Wat Tyler.

Fuller records at the time: 'Now I behold aged Sir Robert buckling on his armour as old Priam at the taking of Troy, but with far better success as proving very victorious.' He must then have been about seventy-five years old, but it was he who helped suppress the revolt and thus saved the king's life, at least for a time. He was in command of the force raised in the city of London by the Lord Mayor, Sir William Walworth, and was beside him when he slew Wat Tyler with his sword. For his outstanding services Sir Robert was honoured by being elected a Freeman of the City of London; and further proof of the gratitude of the citizens of London is expressed in a document still in the archives of the corporation. This was a grant of leave 'to build a Hautpas, to Sir Robert Knolles, and Constance his wife. 5 Ricard II A.D. 1381' – the original is in Norman French.

The hautpas was a bridge some fourteen feet high extending from the house belonging to him and his wife in Seething Lane in the city on the west side, to another house on the east side. The hautpas was built illegally in 1370 by Constance his wife during Sir Robert's absence abroad, '… they rendering yearly unto the Chamberlain of the Guildhall … one red rose, at the Feast of St John the Baptist [24th June], called the Nativity.' Today this beautiful ceremony is carried out by the Company of Watermen & Lightermen who now organize the annual payment of one red rose.

The author has been greatly privileged to be able to quote in their own words details of the ceremony which was 'revived and invigorated between the wars by the late Revd P.B. (Tubby) Clayton, CH, MC, DD, Vicar of All Hallows-by-the-Tower and Founder Padre of Toc H. At the Padre's invitation the Ceremony has been arranged by the Company of Watermen & Lightermen of the River Thames since 1960.'

> *The Ceremony*. What was doubtless a legal formality has now become a most interesting ceremony and one of the City's traditions. The Company of Watermen & Lightermen, which organizes the annual payment of the rose, is based at its Hall in St Mary-at-Hill, which was built in 1780 and is the only remaining Georgian Hall in the City. Coincidentally Sir Robert Knollys acquired in 1402 34 shops and other property in the parish of St Mary-at-Hill which he settled on the Pontefract Hospital. The Ceremony takes place at the Mansion House where the Chief Escort to the Rose – a leading Citizen of London or another distinguished person – presents a red rose to the Lord Mayor. The rose is picked from the Corporation's garden in Seething Lane on the site of the property acquired by Sir Robert and Lady Knollys. The garden was once owned by the Port of London Authority with which the Company has close connections. It is presented to the Lord Mayor on the altar cushion of All Hallows-by-the-Tower church.

The penalty imposed by the Lord Mayor arose from Lady Knollys rashly acting without planning permission from the city of London in the year 1370 during Sir Robert's absence abroad fighting the wars. Their house was in Seething Lane near the Tower of London. She became increasingly angry at the amount of dust borne by the wind from across the other side. As she was a very headstrong woman she acted drastically by buying up the land on which a threshing mill stood, causing all the trouble; and ordered a hautpas (Norman French for footbridge) to be built from one side of Seething Lane to the other. She is said to have created a rose garden in the new portion of land. Sir Robert's house was later occupied by Samuel Pepys. There is still a small rose garden in Seething Lane from which the annual red rose for the presentation is plucked, if it is a perfect, unblemished rose.

On the appointed day, the presentation of the Knollys Rose is carried out with much pageantry. A guard of honour is formed by the bargemaster and the eight winners of the celebrated Doggett's Coat and Badge Race organized by the Company of Watermen & Lightermen of the River Thames. At the Mansion House the Lord Mayor and Lady Mayoress are in attendance by their dual thrones. The verger of the church of All Hallows-by-the-Tower bears an unblemished red rose on a blue altar cushion, accompanied by the chief escort to the Rose (always a chosen person of eminence in the city). The chief escort, after a short speech, then presents the rose to the Lord Mayor. The procession includes the master and clerk of the Company of Watermen & Lightermen and the vicar of All Hallows-by-the-Tower.

Sir Robert died 15 August 1407, recorded as being ninety-two years of age. He requested to be buried beside his wife in the Church of the White Friars in Fleet Street, London, to which church he had been a more than generous benefactor. With his vast wealth from the wars, he had practically rebuilt the church of the White Friars and the churches of Harpley and Sculthorpe in Norfolk. Other beneficiaries were the College and Almshouses at Pontefract in Yorkshire, called Knolles' Hospital, commonly known as the Trinities since the two other founders were Sir Hugh Calverley and Captain Hackwood. He had originally intended to build a hospital near Sculthorpe, but decided to build one at Pontefract.

His greatest achievement, however, was the rebuilding of Rochester Bridge in Kent. In 1387 the French had built a very large fleet at Sluys for an invasion. Fearing that the landing would occur on the south coast the English had destroyed the original bridge over the Medway, a wide river with very strong currents making it dangerous for small boats to navigate. The river cut the highway from Dover to London. On his return to England, Sir Robert Knolles was forced to ferry his troops, horses and baggage after finding the bridge had been swept away. He urgently petitioned the king for permission to rebuild it, promising to pay all the costs required so to do, 'and to hold lands in memoriam thereof.' The king, with the assent of Parliament, agreed.

This still famous bridge, destroyed in 1856, together with its chapel was completed one year before Sir Robert's death. The bridge was stated by its builders to be '566 feet one inch and half a quarter of an inch long and fifteen feet wide', and it was considered superior to all others in England except London Bridge. The chapel at the east end of the bridge was called Allesolven chapel by the express wish of its founder Sir John Cobham, and had three chaplains to pray for the souls of Sir John Cobham, Sir Robert Knolles and many others connected with the building of both bridge and chapel. Sir Robert Knolles left two wills, one in Latin and one in English and died without issue. He was a great soldier and a great man, 'Just and liberal to his soldiers and shared their quarters and privations.' His memory is kept alive today, after six hundred years, by the presentation of an unblemished red rose in one of the most beautiful ceremonies in the city of London.

THE TICHBORNE FAMILY

THE ANNUAL DOLE

One of the most remarkable stories in the history of Hampshire is that of the legendary Tichborne Dole. The family is also renowned for the celebrated Tichborne Claimant trial in 1871 in which a professed Australian butcher claimed to be the heir to the title, estates and family mansion, Tichborne House a claim which he lost. The trial cost £200,000 in legal charges, £80,000 of which the Tichbornes had to pay.

Tichborne is about one-and-a-quarter miles from Alresford in Hampshire and the manor has been held continuously since the twelfth century. The legend of the dole originated in the reign of Henry II when Sir Roger de Tichborne married Mabella, an extremely wealthy lady from the Isle of Wight. When she was dying from a wasting disease she earnestly requested her husband to arrange that a small part of their extensive estates should be set aside to produce sufficient corn for an annual gift of bread to the poor of the parish. She had all her life been a philanthropist, generous and warm-hearted for charity and especially gifts for the poor. Now that her very considerable dowry had become her husband's as was customary in those times she was forced to beg him so that her generosity could continue.

Her husband agreed to her last wish only on his own terms, certain that she would not be able to carry them out. He snatched a lighted brand from the fire and told her that all the ground she could cover holding it aloft before it became extinguished should be used for her charity. To his astonishment and dismay, ill as Mabella was she determined to carry out the task and the lighted brand was placed in her hand. Only by divine assistance could she have achieved what she set out to do, covering no less than twenty-five acres of land before the brand became extinguished. Down to this very day the area is known as 'The Crawls'.

Her death followed shortly but before that she solemnly warned her husband that if her wish were not carried out and the dole of bread for the poor was not administered each Lady Day the Tichborne family would become extinct. She followed this curse by a prophecy that a generation of seven sons would be followed by a generation of seven daughters and the family name would be changed.

The Tichborne Dole, once established by the wishes of Lady Mabella, continued for some six hundred years until it became so well-known that visitors started coming from all over the country to take part in it. Booths and stalls were set up, a fair organized, vagrants and beggars became a nuisance. The recipients of the bread were persuaded to sell it for money. It became so serious that Sir Henry Tichborne, the 7th Baronet, decided to put an end to what was becoming a menace – the charity later resuming, distributing flour in place of loaves.

It is questionable if what he did was in any way a breach of the original agreement, but he decided, as the family had always been devout Roman Catholics, that he would make a charity to the church. The ceremony would be blessed by the priest offering prayers for the soul of Lady Mabella, one in Latin and one in English. The loaves of bread were changed to flour. Nineteen hundred loaves had been distributed until 1796. These were changed and measured out as one-and-three-quarter tons of flour, to be distributed to the poor of Tichborne and Cheriton only. The maximum allocation to be given to a family of six was twenty-eight lbs. All eligible recipients were to be selected by a steward.

After the chaplain had blessed the flour with a symbolic sprinkling of holy water the medieval Tichborne dole weight was used to measure the flour. Any that was left over went by traditional right to the Dowager Lady Tichborne. This distribution is carried out annually on Lady Day 25 March down to this day. Permission to attend can be made on application to the Southern Tourist Board, Town Hall Centre, Eastleigh, Hampshire.

The step taken by Sir Henry Tichborne aroused fear amongst the inhabitants of the two villages who were all aware of the legendary curse. Sir Henry already had three sons and four more were to come. Within a century every detail of the prophecy would be achieved – seven daughters and a change in the family name – as well as a totally unexpected disaster for the Tichbornes.

The 9th Baronet took the surname of Doughty from a Miss Doughty, a wealthy lady with estates in Lincolnshire and Surrey. She left everything to Edward, third son of Sir Henry, on the condition that her name should precede his own. When he died his brother, the 10th Baronet, had Royal Licence to acquire the name as Sir James Francis Doughty-Tichborne. He had two sons, Roger Charles and Alfred. The death of their father in 1862 led to one of the most celebrated trials in English legal history, known as the Tichborne Claimant Trial.

It happened because Roger Charles, as a result of his bitter disappointment over a love-affair, had decided to go abroad. Ten years before his father's death he made his will, placed it in a sealed envelope, and set out for Paris where his parents were staying to wish them farewell. He took ship in the *Bella*, bound for Valparaiso. Nothing more was ever heard of him or the ship. It was naturally presumed by the family that he was dead and Alfred was now heir to the title.

They had not reckoned with his mother, however. Lady Tichborne stubbornly refused to believe that Roger was dead and at once began inserting advertisements in all the papers for any information concerning her son and the ship.

It was eight years before she received an answer and that from Australia. The writer informed her that he was the claimant to the Tichborne title and estates. Lady Tichborne at once sent him money for the passage home. Incredible as it seems, she was at once convinced that the man who came to her was her son, in spite of the fact that he was fat, massive, and weighed thirty stone.

The trustees naturally wanted to meet him, informing

him and his mother that they did not for the moment recognize him as a Tichborne or having a claim to the title. The claimant, fully supported by Lady Tichborne, at once took legal action against the trustees and so began a trial, or rather two trials, that cost £200,000, an enormous sum in those days.

The hearing began in May 1873 and lasted until February 1874, in the course of which it emerged that the Claimant was a Wapping butcher named Arthur Orton. On the 103rd day he 'elected to be non-suited' and was therefore ordered to be sent to trial for perjury. The whole country became divided over the claimant's cause. Some felt 'he was a man deprived of his rights'. His own learned counsel, Dr Kennedy, firmly believed that the claimant believed he was the rightful heir. At the trial for perjury the judge sentenced him to fourteen years penal servitude. The claimant died in 1898 and was buried with a brass plate claiming that he was 'Sir Roger Charles Doughty-Tichborne'.

The Tichbornes had been almost bankrupted by the costs of the trial yet their misfortunes still continued. The family mansion was so severely damaged by fire that it had to be rebuilt with materials from the original house.

The story is also told of an earlier curse, evidence of which is in the Tichborne chapel in the parish church – a fifteenth-century figure of the fourteen-year-old Richard Tichborne who died as the result of a curse put upon him by a gypsy.

4 *Curses*

THE LAMBTON FAMILY

THE WORM

'No earlier owners of Lambton are on record than the ancient and honourable family which still bears the local name.' So wrote the historian and antiquary Robert Surtees of their lineage. According to *Burke's Peerage* their lineage has been proved by attestation and individual witnesses to charters proving their line to be 'from a period very nearly approaching the Norman Conquest.' After eight centuries they were created first a baron in 1828 and elevated as Earls of Durham in 1833, the first of whom was the statesman known as 'King Jog' to his enemies, 'jogging along on forty thousand a year.' He was the aristocratic radical behind the Reform Bill and creator of Liberal imperialism.

The Lambtons were owners of an ancient castle of which there is no record, then of Old Lambton Hall which was pulled down in 1877 and finally of the present Lambton Castle. This was not built on the site of Old Lambton Hall but incorporated much of the large estates of the Harriton family of Harriton Hall nearby with whom the family intermarried. Lambton Castle's impressive position on the banks of the river Wear is seen at its best from the splendid Lamb Bridge. The castle suffered considerable damage when later it was discovered that it had been built over an ancient, disused and forgotten coal-pit which caused the castle serious subsidence. It is not open to the public but the family is extant.

The legend of the Lambton Worm has never lost its association with the family throughout the centuries. The total impossibility of its existence has never ceased to intrigue writers about this fabulous monster. Its origins may lie with Norse or Danish invaders of England in the remote past. It is noteworthy that credence was given to the legend as late as 1794.

The first member of the family to be involved with the monster that created the legend was John Lambton who, at some remote time, most probably the early Norman period, began the celebrated tradition of the Lambton Worm. He was a notoriously impious man, perhaps giving birth to the local feeling about the family as 'being so brave that they feared neither man nor God'. It was his defiance of God that brought upon his family the curse of a witch. Sir John was a Knight of Rhodes and since the order was founded during the Crusades it is surprising that he repeatedly spent the Sabbath fishing in the river Wear whilst the rest of the people went to church, including his own servants.

He greatly flattered himself upon his skill as an angler. One Sunday, as he sat by the river having a bad time with his rod, cursing and swearing at the lack of a catch, he felt a sudden hard pull on the line. As he began to bring it in he was sure by the weight that he was going to land a fine fish when to his disgust he saw that what was on his hook was not a fish but a most repulsive object. It was more like a large snake, or even a huge worm with two holes each side of its mouth.

At that moment a man was staring at him, having stopped on his way from church. John then asked the stranger to have a look at his catch and tell him what he thought it was. The stranger peered for a short time, confirmed that it had two holes each side of its mouth, crossed himself, said that whatever it was boded no good for Lambton and went on his way home. John Lambton threw the creature into the well nearby. Soon afterwards Lambton went off for seven years on the Crusades against the infidels, doubtless forgetting all about the strange thing he had caught that Sunday morning.

During the seven years of his absence the countryside round Lambton Castle was devastated and the people terrified by the repulsive worm, or serpent, or more probably dragon, that had been flung down the well. It had grown to an immense length, selecting for its chosen lair a small hill, still known as Worm Hill, on the north side of the River Wear, about a mile-and-a-half below the castle. Such was its strength and length that it could wind its coils three times round the hill, whose circumference was said to be three hundred yards.

From this chosen site the Worm, as it was called from the very beginning, preyed upon flocks of sheep and herds of cattle, its poisonous breath killing the pastures. The frightened people tried desperately hard to pacify it by troughs of milk from nine cows every day. This last was a custom relating to dragons carried out in many other places. As the attacks increased, daring knights who had tried unsuccessfully to slay it were torn to pieces by this uncanny monster. Such was the situation when John Lambton returned from abroad, determined to do battle with the Worm. His first decision was to consult a witch.

Throughout the centuries belief in witches has always been very deep. The belief in the power of a witch was used by William the Conqueror against Hereward the Wake in the siege of Ely Abbey. Equally shared was a belief in monsters such as the Worm and in the Devil himself. It was not surprising, therefore, that John Lambton decided to consult a witch for advice on how to deal with this terror. The first thing the witch did was to reprimand him for causing all the trouble when he had it in his power to kill it when he had hooked it, a charge he countered by assuring her he thought he had really caught the Devil.

She then directed him how to destroy the monster. He was to have a suit of armour made, covered with spear-blades which combined with his longsword could kill it; but, she warned him, her advice was conditional upon him taking a vow that after destroying the monster he would give three horn blasts, then kill the first living thing he met. If he failed to keep his word, she solemnly warned him, 'Lords of Lambton for nine generations would not die in their beds.' He swore he would keep his promise and left her, to begin all preparations for putting an end to the Worm. Other knights helped him to make the armour. He registered his vow of repentance in the chapel, now demolished, near the fifteenth-century Bridgeford Bridge.

His battle when it began was long, hard, and very dangerous, for immediately the monster saw him approaching it uncoiled its vast length with amazing rapidity and was the first to attack. The more sword wounds it received the greater was its fury. Those parts of its body that had been severed immediately reunited. Finally launching its great weight at its opponent it wound itself round Lambton's body like a huge python in order to crush its prey to death. The attack would have succeeded had not the spear-blades cut deeply into its coils, forcing it to release Lambton before it made suddenly for the river to drink. It was a fatal move, for Lambton quickly saw that his sword cuts had severed parts of its body so that they no longer reunited, so he struck again and again with his sword. The monster began to float downstream until the whole of its body was severed and it suddenly drowned.

The whole operation had taken most of the day and Lambton climbed exhausted out of the water. Then remembering the warning words of the witch he gave three triumphant blasts on his horn as a signal of victory. He had arranged with his old father that his hound would hear it and was to be released at once, but after waiting anxiously he saw his father hurrying towards him, out of breath and saying that he could not wait to be the first to greet him. Unable to kill his father, as the first living thing he met, he sent him back to unleash the hound before killing it with his sword.

It is interesting to note the remarks made by Robert Surtees when Old Lambton Hall was pulled down in 1877. In the garden there were found stone relics of two figures, possibly sixteenth century, one feminine, the other a knight in curious armour, studded with sharp blades, engaged in battle with a strange monster. He obviously represented John Lambton slaying the worm. The figures were later moved into Lambton Castle where they are still said to be.

John Lambton's failure to fulfil his vow and slay the *first* living creature he saw after his three blasts on his horn to signify victory resulted in the witch's terrible curse on nine generations of the Lambton family being carried out.

The chief authority on the manner and place of death of the heirs of the Lambtons is Sir Bernard Burke of *Burke's Peerage* and *Burke's Landed Gentry*, yet even with his vast erudition in heraldry and genealogy there is still confusion. It is certain that a number of them did die bedless, as the witch had prophesied. The fear of doing so lasted well into the mid-eighteenth century when great curiosity arose in the lifetime of Henry Lambton to know 'if the curse would hold good to the end.' It seems to have done so since he died in his carriage when crossing the new bridge in 1761.

His brother, the celebrated Major-General John Lambton, succeeded to the title, representing Durham through six Parliaments and marrying into the distinguished Strathmore family. The motto under their coat of arms is a very significant one, 'Le Jour Viendra' (The day will come). One might wonder if this had anything to do with the witch's curse.

The major-general was not himself convinced that the curse of the Lambton Worm had positively ended with his brother's death. So determined was he that he would not die bedless that during his last illness he kept a horse-whip close to his bed, 'fearful that the prophecy might be fulfilled by his servants under the idea that he could not die in his bed and thus elude the prediction.' He died peacefully in his bed in 1794. There is no recorded evidence that the curse on the nine generations was carried further into the family, but the legend of the famous Lambton Worm seems as imperishable as all good legends should be.

THE LINDSAYS

THE PRODIGAL

The Lindsays, Earls of Crawford, were at the height of their power second only to the royal Stuarts. They affected a royal state of dignity with their own courts, herald, chamberlain, chaplain, secretary, pages, esquires, all specially trained in matters dealing with chivalry, even their domestic servants were of noble birth. They were enormously wealthy with vast estates and castles, including twenty lordships and baronies throughout Scotland. Throughout the thirteenth, fourteenth and fifteenth centuries, it was inconceivable that their power could ever be threatened, yet suddenly they were reduced almost to ruin. In a living legend, their fortunes slowly recovered and they are today premier earls of Scotland.

The first cause of their tragic change of fortune came by the rashness and extravagance of David Lindsay, 12th Earl, known by all as 'The Prodigal' who recklessly and arrogantly alienated all the possession of the earldom that some solution had to be found. It was made worse by the fact that he had no son, so that all the family agnates (descendants both male and female of the ancestor of their lineage) held a solemn council at which it was agreed to have him imprisoned until his death. He was therefore imprisoned in Edinburgh Castle where he died on 5 February 1621.

He left an orphan daughter, the Lady Jean, as his heiress. So bitter and callous were the feelings and conduct of those who had sent her father to his death in prison that they left her destitute and uncared for. Such was the depth of her humiliation that she was given no education whatsoever, nor were clothes provided for her so that she was soon on the streets as a gypsy or tinker until a crier found her and the two eloped. He left her soon afterwards and she lived entirely by beggary until, with the restoration of King Charles II, notice was given to him of the terrible fate of such a noble and well-born child. He at once granted her a pension for life.

Edzell Castle, built in Norman times, had been the home of the Lindsays, though much repaired and restored during the seventeenth century at such great expense by the prodigal 12th Earl as, according to an inscription on one of the walls, 'caused him to die in extraordinary debt.' A very remarkable legend has sprung up about the castle and the David Lindsay who lived there for a very long time after the Prodigal's death. It was said that he had been finally driven out of his castle by the terrible curse put upon him and his wife by an embittered gypsy. She had been the mother of two dumb children who had been caught by one of Lindsay's keepers poaching in the castle grounds. They had been sentenced to death by hanging. Half-crazed by fear and horror of the deed the gypsy woman had come to the castle to scream out at the master a most terrible curse.

> By all the Demons of Hell I curse you! For you, Lady Crawford, you shall not see the sun set, you and the unborn babe you carry will both be buried in the same grave; and for you, Lord Crawford, you shall die a death that would make the boldest man ever born of a woman, even to witness, shriek with fear.

There are two versions of what happened to David Lindsay. One is that he abandoned the castle almost at once, though there is no evidence of his wife dying before sunset on the day of the curse. With what was left of his wrecked fortune he bought a small estate somewhere in the north of Scotland, before he was forced to sell what he had 'and landless and a homeless outcast he retired to the Orkney Islands where he became a hostler in an inn at Kirkwall where he died at the age of eighty in 1744'. Another version of his end is that he was devoured by wolves, a death which bore out the last terrible words of the gypsy's curse.

It is after this that the Lindsay Crawford lineage becomes extremely complicated. Alexander Lindsay, 4th Earl of Balcarres, a representative Peer for Scotland 1734–6, became heir-male of the Lindsays, a position which thus became reunited to the arms and chiefship which had devolved in terms of the entail of the Earldom of Crawford.

Today, after a remarkable change in their fortunes, the Earls of Crawford are now the premier earls of Scotland, and, if their claims to the Dukedom of Montrose were admitted, they would be also the premier dukes of Scotland. Their ancient home, Edzell Castle, forfeited when the family supported the Old Pretender in 1715, rapidly deteriorated. What remained of it came under the protection of HM Office of Works in 1934 and is open to the public.

THE MACKENZIES

THE SEAFORTH CURSE

The Seaforth curse, issued by the Warlock of the Glen, is one of the most dramatic of all those legends that have extinguished great historic families such as the Mackenzies. The origin of many of the ancient Scottish families are often speculative, but according to one authority the Mackenzies were descended from Colin FitzGerald, a cadet from the ancient Irish house of Geraldine who, driven out of his own country, sought refuge in Scotland; receiving from Alexander III, in 1266, the first free feudal barony of Kintail.

Their splendid, simple and ancient coat of arms is a stag's head caboshed (clean cut). It is said that this originated from Colin's son Kenneth, who, succeeding him as 2nd Baron, later saved this king's life from a stag at bay whilst out hunting one day. He cut off its head with one blow from his sword, whence he was known as 'Caberfeidh', or stag's head. It is blazoned in heraldry as 'azure a stag's head caboshed or' (on a blue background a gold stag's head). He became a powerful and a popular chief with two great castles. One was Eilean Donan Castle, near Dornie, Wester Ross; the other, the famous Brahan Castle near Dingwall, in one of the most northerly Scottish counties and the place where the great drama of the Seer's curse took place.

By a curious coincidence each of the first six feudal barons had only one son as successor to the title. Such was their power that they virtually ruled the northern Highlands, increasing their wealth, estates and titles until in 1623 Lord Mackenzie's son Colin was created Earl of Seaforth. They were all fervent loyalists to the causes of Charles I and Charles II, the latter restoring all their estates forfeited to Cromwell. Kenneth, the 3rd Earl, unknowingly began the extinction of the Seaforth line when he married a lady descended from one of his own family. Isabella Mackenzie, daughter of Sir John Mackenzie of Tarbat and sister of the 1st Earl of Cromarty, was a cruel and vindictive woman.

The earl had occasion to visit Paris some time after the restoration of Charles II. As time passed the countess, who had been left in Brahan Castle, grew more restless and even suspicious, for the date of his promised return had long passed. Her anxiety turned now to anger and an even deeper suspicion that caused her to take the fatal step of sending a messenger to Strathpeffer for the renowned seer or Warlock of the Glen, born in Ug, Lewis, in the Western Isles. These seers were more feared than respected for their insight into the future as well as the present. This strange gift of second sight is peculiarly Scottish. The legends of their magic are not only amazing but numerous, even today, no doubt springing from their Celtic blood. It is, however, unfortunate that most of their prophecies are unhappy omens, even warnings.

Lady Mackenzie vindictively chose to arrange that all her vassals and retainers should hear whatever the seer had to say and, as with many legends, there are various versions of the details. When the warlock asked her what she wished from him she told him that the earl had gone to Paris and as he had not returned at his promised time she wanted to know where he was and what he was doing. At first the warlock demurred, which annoyed the countess, then bringing out his strange divining stone he put it to his eyes and remained silent, gazing earnestly into it. He said that the earl seemed to be pleasantly engaged and showed no signs of wishing to return. The countess was furious and demanded more details saying he would be severely punished if he withheld the truth of what he saw.

'Since you force me to tell you', he answered 'what will only make you unhappy I will do so.' He paused but she was now beside herself with suspicion and anger, pestering him to tell her more. He then told her, and the expectant guests, that he had seen the earl in a large and sumptuously furnished Paris salon. On his lap was a most beautiful woman whose hand was pressed to his lips, whilst his arms were round her waist.

In a furious burst of uncontrollable anger she denounced him as a liar, traducer, and defamer of her husband before her vassals and retainers, viciously ordering his immediate execution. She refused absolutely to heed the appeals of all present for mercy and ordered the sentence to be carried out immediately. One version said he was hanged, another that he was to be burned alive in a spiked barrel of tar, but before his death he threw his divining stone into the loch and uttered a terrible curse which Highlanders still talk about.

> I see into the far future and I read the Doom of the race of Seaforth which will end in sorrow and extinction. I see a chief, the last of his house both deaf and dumb, the father of four sons, all of whom he will follow to the grave, and no future chief of the Mackenzie clan shall reside in Brahan or in Kintail. All his possessions shall be inherited by a white-hooded lassie from the East who shall kill her own sister. As a sign all these things shall come to pass there shall be four great lairds in the last days of the chief and dumb Seaforth. One shall be buck-toothed, one hare-lipped, one half-witted and one stammerer.

Every single prophesied word in this terrible curse occurred and in almost 150 years the great line of Seaforth became extinct in the male line. To complete the curse the last male Seaforth's daughter, knowing nothing at all of what had happened returned to Scotland from India after the death of her husband. She wore the white hood of a widow. Later, when driving a pony and trap, she had an accident which resulted in the death of her sister. Even down to this day the legend of the curse has become an integral part of Scottish history and folklore.

Since Countess Isabella Mackenzie was the sister of the 1st Earl of Cromarty, the Mackenzie line continued through the female descent becoming Earls of Cromartie (the spelling changed in 1861). On 13 December 1989 Roderick Mackenzie, 7th Earl of Cromartie died at the age of eighty-five. As Chief of the Mackenzie Clan he was the epitome of all the famous Highland clan chiefs and perhaps the proudest moment in his long and adventurous life was in 1979 when Lyon King of Arms confirmed his claim to be Caberfeidh, chief of Mackenzie, a title dormant since the male Scottish line had died out more than 150 years earlier. This was the honourable title of his ancestor, the 2nd feudal Baron of Kintail, who saved the king's life from a stag at bay.

Rorie Mackenzie was a man of singular courage and determination. He fought as a regular soldier in his own regiment, the Seaforth Highland Regiment in Ulster and on the North-west frontier, retired in 1939, but was called up in 1940 as major of the 4th Battalion of the Seaforths, and was captured a few months later at St Valery together with most of the Highland Division. As a prisoner of war he set about writing his history *Cromartie Highland Life 1850–1914*. He died in his beloved Castle Leod, Ross and Cromarty, a great chief of a great clan.

One of the greatest legacies of the Earl of Seaforth is Eilean Donan Castle, near Dornie, Wester Ross. It is almost the perfect castle, solidly set on a promontory where three sea lochs meet in what must be one of the most beautiful settings in the world. This impregnable stronghold is held by the powerful Clan MacRae who acted as Constables for the Earls of Seaforth, who also as feudal Barons of Kintail, possessed the nearby Kintail Forest, now the property of the National Trust for Scotland.

The original fortified stronghold built in 1230 was relentlessly attacked by warring clans through almost five centuries until in 1719, after the failure of the Jacobite rising, it was shelled and destroyed by English frigates. Legend has it that Farquhar MacRae had seen in a vision the ruined castle totally restored to its former strength and glory. Between the years 1912 and 1932 his dream was turned into reality by Lt. Col. John McRae-Gilstrap at a cost of a quarter of a million pounds. Every detail of Farquhar's dream was confirmed by plans of the original castle found in Edinburgh Castle. Now that it is open to the public it is an unforgettable experience to see it. Legend has it that the castle took its name from St Donan who had a hermitage here in the very early days when Christianity was brought to the Western Isles. He could never even have imagined such a great castle would be built. Perhaps it was he himself who brought the vision to Farquhar MacRae. The McRaes are still constables of the Earls of Seaforth.

THE MONTACUTES

THE ECCLESIASTICAL CURSE

The English Heritage property of Sherborne Old Castle in Dorset, now ruined, is a twelfth-century castle abandoned after the Civil Wars. It was originally built by Roger, Bishop of Salisbury, between 1107 and 1135. It was built with the stone from an earlier Saxon castle and was granted to the Bishopric in 1078 by Osmond King of Wessex. This fortress stood within vast lands. In order to perpetuate this rich gift Osmond the king placed upon it a unique ecclesiastical curse, every word of which came true through the succeeding centuries. 'Whosever shall take these lands from the bishopric or diminish them in great or in small shall be accursed not only in this world but also in the world to come, unless in his life he make restitution thereof.'

The powerful and autocratic Bishop Roger at once began to build a splendid residential palace, where he was to live in regal state with great wealth, and another castle in Devizes in Wiltshire. His reign of splendour was short-lived for he both defied and opposed the authority of King Stephen (1135–54) during the civil war between him and Matilda of Anjou. The king seized his castle, imposed a heavy fine and exiled the bishop. It was a very early start to the prophetic words of the curse.

For over two hundred years, however, the curse remained dormant until Edward III (1327–77) released it from Crown property and granted it and all its lands to Montacute, Earl of Salisbury. This so infuriated Bishop Wyville that he challenged the earl to mortal combat, the winner to take all possessions. He must indeed have underestimated the military skill and courage of the one-eyed earl who often fought in tournaments, he had lost the other in battle, and, in 1343, actually died of severe bruises in the lists at Windsor. The Bishop's arrogance evidently considered the earl's refusal to fight him was cowardice. To make posterity believe it, he had a splendid incised brass memorial erected in Salisbury Cathedral, showing him, complete with mitre and crozier dominating a tiny figure of the earl clasping what looks like a lance and a shield, above are a few frisky rabbits to indicate the bishop's own right to medieval free warren.

The terrible curse on the castle had begun dramatically and so it was to continue on its relentless course. The 2nd Earl was one of the original Knights of the Garter, founded by Edward III. Tradition says that this was out of love the king had for the Fair Maid of Kent, the earl's wife, who afterwards married the Black Prince. The king held a great ball at Cirencester and when one of the dances had ended and the dancers left the floor, an abandoned lady's garter lay in the centre. No one dared to claim it for fear of the king, but it was he who stepped out, picked up the garter and held it up for all to see. 'This garter will never be forgotten', he cried aloud. 'Honi soit qui mal y pense (Evil be to him who evil thinks), the proud motto of all successive Garter Knights and the Royal Arms. The earl had the misfortune to kill his own son in a joust and died in combat.

He was succeeded by his nephew the 3rd Earl, a great favourite of Richard II (1377–1400). The earl, together with two other loyal Earls of Huntingdon and Kent, plotted to murder Henry IV by dressing as players at Christmas-time in Windsor Castle. The plot was discovered and fleeing by night to Cirencester the people blocked up the town exits and fought with the earls as they tried to escape. The earls yielded, asking to see the king, but as one of their priests had set fire to the town, they were beheaded by the townsmen.

The 4th Earl died during his command of the army at the siege of Orleans. The line of Montacute became extinct by his death in 1421, a double tragedy since all the Sherborne estates and castle had been restored to him by Henry V.

For another two hundred years Sherborne Castle and estates returned to the Church until the dissolution of the monasteries, when it again reverted to the Crown in 1537 and was granted to the Lord Protector, the Duke of Somerset, uncle to King Edward VI. Once again the curse arose from its long sleep, for the Lord Protector was arraigned as a traitor and executed. In 1540 'Bloody' Mary granted it back to the Bishop of Sherborne. In 1591 Elizabeth I deprived the Bishopric, in her ruthless persecution of all Roman Catholics in revenge for 'Bloody' Mary's treatment of the Protestants, and granted it to Sir Walter Raleigh. Wealthy and high in favour with his queen, he later built a beautiful and stately mansion very near to the ruined castle, secretly marrying the celebrated 'Bessie' Throckmorton without the queen's consent. When Elizabeth was informed she summoned Bessie's father Nicholas Throckmorton to Court and severely rebuked him as she stormed at him: 'God's death, Villain, I will have thy head.' to which the statesman and diplomat dared to reply: 'In that case you will do best to consider, madam, how you will keep your own on its shoulders.' In spite of her anger, however, she leased Sherborne Castle to Sir Walter Raleigh. Two years later Raleigh abandoned the old castle and began to build himself a new one, calling it the Lodge. Both he and his wife loved it dearly.

Sadly, in 1618 Raleigh, betrayed by James I to Spain, was confined to the Tower and executed in Palace Yard, Westminster, on 29 October 1618. Even then the curse did not stop.

In spite of the family's complicity in the Gunpowder Plot, Sir John Digby was able to retire to his estate, the Lodge and he set about enlarging it. The curse seems then to have ceased as successive members of the family have improved the Lodge which is today open to the public.

Strange as it may seem, the Bishops of Salisbury have received mysterious death-warnings over the centuries of white birds seen over Salisbury Plain in Wiltshire. Legend has it that these birds, as large as albatrosses according to one witness, had dazzling white wings that did not move. The birds hover over the plain and over the Meadows and Palace Gardens whenever a Bishop of Salisbury is about to die. A detailed account of these white birds was recorded in 1885 and more recently on 11 August 1911, Miss Oliver who saw them on her way home to the palace. They were floating, rather than hovering across the sky. She was with a party of choir-boys from Wilton and as she called out about the birds only one choir-boy saw them before they disappeared. She herself knew nothing about the legend, but when she arrived home the bishop, who had been perfectly fit in the morning when she left, had suddenly died. It was only then that other members of the household told her of the legend.

THE VISCOUNTS MONTAGUE

THE COWDRAY CURSE

The terrifying power of two curses put upon a family that became extinct after just four generations has no greater evidence than in the splendid Tudor ruins of Cowdray House near Midhurst in Sussex, where the distinguished Browne family lived. They were granted Battle Abbey, the richest monastic building in England, together with all its lands, when Henry VIII dissolved the monasteries and religious houses in 1538. A curse fell upon the head of the family, Sir Anthony Browne, whose arrogance, wealth and personal conduct gave great offence to the Benedictine monks.

It was on a night when high revelry, great drinking, noise and ill-behaviour had reached their highest pitch that Sir Anthony summoned the abbot to appear before him and his guests at high table in the refectory. Amidst shouting and laughter the abbot was ordered to vacate the abbey that very night with all his monks. After a long pause the abbot uttered the words that struck silence in the great room as he pronounced the slow and deliberate words of the curse upon the Browne family: 'in sleeping and waking, in eating and drinking in all their incomings and outgoings, until fire and water should destroy their house, and should extinguish their family and all their posterity for ever.' Then, still in a hushed silence, the abbot turned to leave the abbey that night with all his brethren.

Ten years later Sir Anthony Browne died and his son, another Sir Anthony, went to live in Cowdray House, which had been so splendidly built by his half-brother, the Earl of Southampton, who had died in 1543. He must already have been aware of another curse invoked upon the grant of all the lands at Cowdray, including the possession of Easeborne Priory, the nuns having been expelled from the peaceful priory built in 1279. It was the Sub-Prioress of Easebourne who invoked the first curse, the curse of heaven upon the male line of the Browne family 'by fire and by water' which came to pass four centuries later. He, like all his descendants, were staunch Roman Catholics and he was created 1st Viscount Montague by 'Bloody' Queen Mary.

His son, the 2nd Viscount, was the first to be struck by the curse, for he was deeply involved in the Gunpowder

Plot during the reign of James I, narrowly escaping execution by being imprisoned in the Tower and paying a huge fine. Francis Browne, 3rd Viscount, suffered even more from the curse for he became involved in the Civil War on the losing side having all his vast estates, including Battle Abbey, sequestrated by the roundheads who garrisoned Cowdray House. Later this was captured by the royalists, and narrowly escaped destruction.

Francis Browne, the 4th Viscount Montague, seems to have been a legendary figure with a most violent temper involving him in numerous legends still extant, notably when he shot the priest dead in Cowdray Chapel for starting to hold Mass before the viscount had entered to hear it. The 7th Viscount did a great deal to improve the Cowdray estates, kept a pack of buck-hounds and was visited by Dr Johnson who is recorded as having said: 'I should like to have stayed at Cowdray four and twenty hours. We see here how our ancestors lived.'

The 8th and last Viscount, George Samuel, seems to have been especially selected for the full effects of the curse that had been smouldering throughout the lives of the previous seven. In the summer of 1793 the young viscount was only twenty-five years old when he set out with a friend to try and shoot the dangerous Schaffhausen rapids in a flat-bottomed boat, evading the police who wished to prevent the event. They succeeded in shooting the first fall but disaster struck them at the second. They were drowned and buried at Laufenburg. The Swiss police at once sent a messenger to Cowdray House to inform his sister of the tragedy. The messenger met another sent by the sister to inform her brother that Cowdray House had been gutted and ruined by fire; 'fire and water' as the curse had predicted. She had married William Stephen Poyntz, of that ancient and illustrious family, who also became part of the curse, perhaps the most vicious since he was not even a Montague, but the abbot of Battle Abbey had included the posterity of the Brownes.

The Poyntzs had two sons who together with their father and mother went for a holiday in Bognor. The year was 1815 and on a warm and sunny day Mr Poyntz decided he would take the two boys out in a boat. Mrs Poyntz, never forgetting the power of the curse upon her family, pleaded with him not to do so and watched unhappily as he refused to listen to her.

There was not a cloud in the sky and he saw no danger in what he was doing, until suddenly a storm broke over them, upsetting the boat and forcing them to swim for their lives; the two boys were drowned. Mrs Poyntz never recovered from the shock, dying five years later and all three are buried in the family vault at Easebourne. Mr Poyntz died from a hunting accident a few years later, thus completing the curse in every detail.

The Cowdray estates were bought by Sir Weetman Dickinson Pearson Bt, later created 1st Viscount Cowdray. It was he who carried out the restoration of the splendid ruins of Cowdray House which are today open to the public.

THE PHILLIPSONS

THE SKULLS

In a hushed court Myles Phillipson, the magistrate, closed the case brought against the accused, Kraster and Dorothy Cook for stealing. He sentenced them to sequestration of all their property, and imprisonment in Kendal gaol to await the next assizes where further punishment would be meted out, which in those days, theft being a capital charge, carried the sentence of death or transportation for life. As he rose to leave the bench Dorothy Cook stood to issue a most terrible curse on the magistrate and all his family, in words that have become a legend in the history of what was then Westmorland and is now Cumbria.

> Guard thyself Myles Phillipson; Thou thinkest thou hast managed grandly but that tiny lump of land is the dearest a Phillipson will ever possess; for you will never prosper, neither your breed. Whatsoever scheme you undertake will wither in your hand. The side you take will always lose. The time will come when the Phillipsons will not own an inch of land, and while Calgarth Hall stands we'll haunt it night and day. Never will ye be rid of us.

The prophecy of Dorothy Cook and its fulfilment was as dramatic as it was effective.

Throughout the whole of their history the Phillipsons had been both feared and disliked. A combination of power, wealth, arrogance and brutality had been inherited by each successive heir. They were said to have been a wild, daredevil race. One of them, known as Robin the Devil, was the most reckless of all. He took sides for the king when the Civil Wars broke out, and soon became one of his most dashing, brave and insolent cavaliers, hating the puritans with all his heart. When Colonel Briggs, a parliamentarian, captured Kendal, in the Lake District, he began at once to enforce his religion, as decreed by Cromwell, upon the most unwilling parishioners. Robin the Devil soon made up his mind to deal with the colonel in his own way.

One Sunday morning he set out at the head of a troop of horses to teach this upstart roundhead a lesson he would not forget, and to kill him if he caught him alive, even in Kendal church itself. Fortunately for the colonel he was not at the service, so that he did not see the troop of horses ride up to and surround the church. Robin the Devil stormed in, brandishing his drawn sword, swaggering and shouting up and down the nave, terrifying the congregation and causing excitement and confusion. Sir Walter Scott, a guest many years later of Bishop Watson at Calgarth Hall, who had purchased it after the ruin of the Phillipsons in 1805, wrote of this event in his *Rokeby*.

Despite all the acres of land the Phillipsons had round

Calgarth Hall, Myles Phillipson still found a major problem that had to be solved. This was caused by a small farmhouse within an acre of land which disturbed his line of vision over Lake Windermere and the surrounding beautiful country.

The farm belonged to Kraster and Dorothy Cook and had been in her family for a very long time indeed. They were both poor and very hard-working, for their farm meant everything to them. They had no idea that Phillipson had sworn to get hold of it by whatever means, even force, so they were naturally surprised when one day he called on them with a proposal to buy the farm and the land, which they at once declined. Phillipson renewed his offer week after week, increasing it each time, but still they refused and were now seriously worried by his determination, for he had a bad local reputation of greed and ruthlessness and might easily find ways and means, even illegally, of securing what he wanted. One day, he appeared before them in a jovial and coaxing mood which they instinctively distrusted. Instead of making yet another offer, he came to invite them to a Christmas Eve dinner he was giving to his tenants, and to which he thought they would like to come. Although they were uneasy, they thought it would be better to accept.

Upon arriving at the hall they were even more disturbed when they saw more 'gentry' there than tenants. The table glittered with glass and silver and great bowls of flowers. Most of the guests were in evening dress which made matters worse since they themselves wore only simple country clothes. Phillipson himself greeted them profusely, filled their glasses, introduced them to his wife and other guests and seemed to be a changed man. As they sat at table there was a magnificent silver goblet before them, so beautiful that Dorothy Cook felt compelled to express her feelings to Mrs Phillipson, who seemed to be especially delighted at such a compliment. After dinner there were games, charades and dancing which would go on far into Christmas Day, so the Cooks asked to be excused as they had work to do on the farm, even on Christmas Day and left quite late, led to the door by Phillipson himself who thanked them for coming.

On Boxing Day Kraster saw two men approaching the farm who knocked on the door. As he opened it they pushed past him and showed him a search warrant. When he enquired the reason they said he would soon find out and began searching the house. Both Kraster and Dorothy, who had now joined him, dared say nothing for one did not argue with constables. They heard the men stamping about upstairs, moving furniture, throwing things about while they waited, nonplussed and afraid. The constables came down at last holding out the silver goblet Dorothy had so admired at the Christmas Eve dinner party. They were charged then and there with robbery, arrested, and led away to the gaol to await trial.

The Phillipsons held another great Christmas Eve party a year later, following the sentence of death passed on Kraster and Dorothy Cook at the assizes. Their farmhouse had been demolished and the land was now in the possession of Phillipson. The curse, uttered by Dorothy Cook at the trial began that very night, for Mrs Phillipson who had gone upstairs to dress, came screaming from the room and shouting for help. There on the top step of the staircase were two grinning skulls. There was consternation in Calgarth Hall as news of it spread to the arriving guests. The festivities had to be abandoned, the guests all left, and the skulls remained on the stairs until Phillipson himself carried them out into the garden to be buried the next day. His wife was distraught and angry, refusing to stay in the house that night, but it was too late to go anywhere.

On Christmas Day Phillipson took the two skulls a great distance from the hall and buried them. They returned the same night. They were reburied in a different place but again they returned. They were thrown into Lake

Windermere but after a short time were once more at the head of the staircase. Over the next weeks and months the skulls were continually returning, as Dorothy had prophesied: 'You will never be rid of us.' Finally in an act of desperation Phillipson pounded them to dust and actually scattered the ashes at a great distance from the hall outside the county. Still they returned with all the cruel deliberation of poltergeists, but whereas the identities of most poltergeists are unknown, Myles Phillipson must surely have remembered the words of the curse passed on him and his family – 'As long as Calgarth Hall stands we shall haunt you.'

Stories of the skulls were circulating all over the county, all the servants left the hall, Phillipson's business deals began to fall off, even fail. All efforts to sell the hall and the grounds failed when prospective tenants, even from afar, became aware of the hauntings. Finally Phillipson became bankrupt and died of shock. Within five minutes of his death the most terrible and frightening screams echoed and re-echoed throughout Calgarth Hall. They were so harrowing that they were heard by neighbours far away, but no one dared move to help. The screams went on and on in the deserted hall as if in triumph, for Mrs Phillipson had long ago left it, dying herself shortly after thus fulfilling every word of the Calgarth curse.

The well-known Dr Watson, Bishop of Llandaff, occupied the hall while seeking a smaller house for himself, so enchanted was he by the beauty of the Lake District. He was fully aware of the story of the skulls, and for the benefit of himself and any future purchaser, he carried out a service of exorcism on Calgarth Hall. From that moment all was quiet. No report has ever come since of the haunting of the two skulls of Kraster and Dorothy Cook.

THE STRATHMORES

THE GLAMIS CURSE

The impressive fourteenth-century Glamis Castle is the oldest inhabited castle in Scotland. For six centuries it was the home of the ancestors of the Queen Mother who spent much of her childhood there. She was the Lady Elizabeth Bowes-Lyon, youngest daughter of the fourteenth Earl of Strathmore, before her marriage to the Duke of York who later became George VI after the abdication of Edward VII. The Castle was first built in 1371, but between the years 1650 and 1696 it was remodelled in the French-chateau style by the third Earl of Strathmore.

There is probably no other castle in the world that has been more haunted, more discussed, caused more speculation and even investigation than Glamis, notably for its double legend of a terrible family curse and for its mysterious secret room, the actual whereabouts of which is still unknown. Shakespeare gave the title of Thane of Glamis to Macbeth and it was in the castle that tradition says King Duncan was murdered in a room called Duncan's Hall. Macbeth's sword and coat of mail are still in the castle armoury. The tradition is in conflict with another, that much later a King Malcolm was assassinated in a room known as King Malcolm's Chamber where his bloodstains remained until the floor-boarding was covered over.

It was in 1372, during the reign of King Robert II of Scotland, that Sir John Lyon, feudal Baron of Forteviot, married Joanna, the King's daughter and was granted Glamis for an annual tribute 'of one red-footed falcon to be paid annually on the Feast of Pentecost.' Sir John, known as the White Lyon because of his pale features, was further given the high honour of Great Chamberlain of Scotland.

Sir John brought with him to Glamis a family heirloom known as the Lyon Cup. Such talismans have been classified as lucks, usually cups, vases and bowls and would be jealously preserved by the family. In this case the luck became a doom or an ill-omen, probably because Sir John took it away from the family home instead of leaving it there. From the moment it reached Glamis there was nothing but tragedy throughout the ensuing centuries. Sir John himself, like most of the Scottish clan chieftains had a ferocious and ruthless temper and was the first victim of the supposed luck when he was killed in a duel.

A period of unusual peace followed which was shattered by the tragic drama concerning the 6th Lord Glamis and his wife Janet Douglas, sister of the 6th Earl of Angus, that powerful and equally ruthless, ferocious line, against which the king now vented his implacable anger. After the death of Lord Glamis in 1528, this young and beautiful widow, with her two sons and many relatives, was indicted for attempting to kill James V by witchcraft. On the perjured evidence of her own family and servants Lady Glamis was sentenced to be burned alive on Castle Hill, Edinburgh, in 1537. Her own son John, later the 7th Lord Glamis, was only sixteen at the time. When put to torture to confess his own and his mother's guilt he was so cruelly treated that he also gave false witness against her. His brother George was imprisoned with him.

It is the ghost of this Lady Glamis which has been seen hovering above the clock tower. She is enclosed within a red glow, as if the flames which burned her to death were still alight. John was himself reprieved when James V died and luckily had all the forfeited honours restored to him. His son, the 8th Lord Glamis, was in the most bitter feud with the two clans of Ogilvy and Lindsay. He was killed in an ambush by a member of the latter family.

So bitter was the endless feud between the three clans that tradition says one Lord Glamis, who may well have been the eighth of the line, one day opened the castle gates to admit some of the Ogilvys being hotly pursued by the Lindsays. There was nothing friendly or hospitable in this action for he had them shut up in the dungeons where they were left to starve to death. The grim story relates that the victims actually ate the flesh from their own limbs and that their bones lay strewn about the cells for many years afterwards. It is small wonder the dungeons are haunted to this very day.

The grimmest legend of all must surely be that of an heir who was born misshapen, with tiny arms, legs like a dwarf and no neck. Whoever or whatever the monster was, it was sealed up within the castle walls, the secret guarded to this day.

Somewhere within those sixteen-foot thick walls, near the chapel or in the tower, is hidden the greatest mystery of all in Glamis. It is the legendary secret room. Sir Walter Scott who was staying in the castle wrote of it thus: 'It contains a monument of the peril of feudal times the entrance of which by the law or custom of the family must only be known to three persons at once, viz the Earl of Strathmore, his heir apparent and any third person whom they may take into their confidence.' Augustus Hare in *The Story of My Life* confirmed this when he wrote: '... in the depths of the wall is another chamber more ghastly even than Duncan's Hall, with a secret transmitted from the fourteenth century, which is always known to three persons. When one of the triumvirate dies the successors are compelled by a terrible oath to elect a successor ... all attempts to discover the secret chamber have failed.

Both Bishop Forbes and the Rev Robert Liddell, vicar of St Paul's, Knightsbridge, London, offered to hold a service of exorcism when requested to do so by a Lady Strathmore but her husband had refused. His reply to his wife was extremely grave: 'It is fortunate that you do not know the secret and can never know it, for if you did you would not be a happy woman.' Augustus Hare records: 'Every succeeding Lady Strathmore, Fatima-like, has spent her time tapping at walls, taking up boards and otherwise attempting to discover the secret chamber, but all have failed.'

Nothing on earth would induce the castle factor to stay in the castle at night. Once when a sudden snowstorm cut off the road leading to his house, which was nearly a mile away across the park, he insisted on rousing the gardeners and stablemen to dig out a path, which they were forced to do.

Lord Halifax tells the story of an incident which might have divulged the secret chamber to an outsider. In 1865, when Claude, 13th Earl of Strathmore was in London, a workman in the castle came upon a door leading to a long passage. He went along it some way, then unaccountably became so alarmed that he ran back, reporting what he had seen to the clerk of works. When the factor was told he immediately ordered all work to stop, then telegraphed to the earl in London and to the family lawyer in Edinburgh. The two men hurried as fast as they could to Glamis, thoroughly and severely examining the workman about what he had seen. Finally the man was induced to accept a sufficiently large sum of money for him and his family to emigrate, and to give his word of honour he would never reveal to anyone what he had seen. Lord Halifax, a relative and guest at the time, says the earl became a changed man, silent, moody, with an anxious, scared face.

A story is also told that some years ago, when the Earl of Strathmore was out with a shooting-party, several of the young guests, led by the countess herself, decided to try and discover the secret room. From every window in the castle they hung towels, or cloths, or some other material, then assembled in the grounds to see if there was a window with nothing fluttering from it. Suddenly one of the guests noticed a window high up in the tower with no towel hanging out. Excitedly they all moved towards the tower, only to discover first one, then another, then a third and a fourth window all without towels. But all the doors of the tower were so firmly bolted and barred that entry was impossible. The earl, who had unexpectedly returned was infuriated and expressed his displeasure to the countess in no uncertain terms.

Variations of the legend continue over the centuries down to the present day. In the last century, locals believed that the 14th Earl, father of the Queen Mother, when on his twenty-first birthday he was due to be one of the traditional triumvirate to take the oath of secrecy regarding the secret room, categorically refused to take part in it.

5 *Lucks*

In the legendary history of ancient families there are a few who have been associated with a fascinating and curious kind of talisman known as a luck, the preservation of which ensures the continuity of that family. It is therefore to be guarded most carefully, hidden in a vault, or a safe deposit, or, in one case, in the Bank of England. A luck could be a glass beaker or goblet, a glass bowl, even a brass tray, a horn or a trumpet. Each heir would be informed of its importance to the family when he became the head of it. Five such lucks have belonged to Cumbrian families.

The MacLeod Clan of Dunvegan Castle in the Isle of Skye, Scotland possess a truly unique luck, the Fairy Flag.

THE CURWENS

THE LUCK OF WORKINGTON HALL

Another luck, known as the luck of Workington Hall was a royal gift as was the Muncaster luck. It was given to Sir Henry Curwen in 1568 by Mary, Queen of Scots when she crossed the Border as a fugitive after the fatal battle of Langside.

Another cup, this time of agate, is still in the possession of the family; and is now in Belle-Isle, Bowness-on-Windermere which is open to the public at certain times.

THE LAMBS

THE LUCK OF BURRELL GREEN

Another luck is preserved in a house between Penrith and Carlisle, formerly occupied by the Lamb family. It is perhaps the strangest of lucks since it is neither a fragile glass goblet nor a bowl, but a large circular brass dish sixteen inches in diameter. It has two circles; the inner one is inscribed with Gothic characters 'Mary, Mother of Jesus, Saviour of Man.' The outer circle in modern characters says:

> If this dish be sold or gi'en,
> Farewell the Luck of Burrell Green.

It seems probable that the last words were inserted by the Lamb family (or others). According to Spelman in his *History of Sacrilege* this would cause despoliation of church property and can only bring evil luck which no family would wish to incur. Truly, a strange twist to the tale.

THE LEGGES

THE LUCK OF WOODSOME HALL

Yet another dubious luck was the luck of Woodsome Hall near Huddersfield, home of the Earl of Dartmouth in the seventeenth century. It is the most curious of all the lucks for it is a brass trumpet with silver mountings, the bell ornamented with cherubs, and bears the inscription 'Simon Beale Londini fecit 1667.' It came into possession of the Legge family in 1730. As late as 1922, however, Lord Dartmouth sent it for auction in London where it fetched seventy-five guineas. It is a total mystery how it became known as a luck for no reason can be given for its purpose. Samuel Pepys nevertheless was acquainted with Beale, maker and trumpeter for he mentions him in his diary as 'a civil man', and as a trumpeter, 'one of Oliver's and now of the King's Guards.' Clearly he both made and blew his own trumpet, but whether he had a son who inherited the luck or not, and what exactly was the function of the trumpet remains a mystery.

THE DE LUCYS

THE HORN OF EGREMONT

Another luck belonged to the ancient family of de Lucy and was known as the horn of Egremont, kept always in the Norman castle of Egremont, now a ruin above the village. Amongst the many honours and privileges of the family was the Forestership of Cumberland. The legend of the horn of Egremont was that Hubert de Lucy arranged to have Eustace de Lucy, the rightful lord, murdered while he was on a crusade abroad, in order to steal the horn and lay claim to all the estates. The plot was discovered, Lord Eustace arrived home and at once blew the horn for all to hear as the rightful lord. Only he and each successive heir could do this. In fear and panic Hubert fled to seek sanctuary in a monastery where he presumably died. The Horn has been called a luck and accepted as such.

The same may apply to the Lyon cup brought to Glamis Castle in Scotland by Sir John Lyon from his former home, which may have broken his luck since he was killed in a duel a few years later. Perhaps it is better to treat it as a doom than a luck.

THE MUSGRAVES

THE LUCK OF EDEN HALL

One of the most famous is the luck of Eden Hall which belonged to the ancient family of Musgrave, whose magnificent mansion on the banks of the river Eden was demolished in 1934. The luck itself, after being in the custody of the Bank of England, is now to be seen in the Victoria and Albert Museum in London. It is a very beautiful beaker or goblet with a flaring rim engraved with a design of green, white, blue and yellow enamels. Authorities have differed as to its origin; southern Spain, Morocco or Syria have been suggested, but it was certainly in the care of the Musgraves during the Middle Ages. It was also kept by them in a curious *cuir bouilli* or boiled leather case, leather used by soldiers in the eleventh century and later to reinforce their shields and plate armour. The case was stamped with the sacred letters IHS and this has led to the supposition that the beaker or goblet was used as a chalice for holy communion.

Even more legendary is the fact of its original discovery in the grounds of Eden Hall by the Musgraves' seneschal. This was the title of a high-ranking household officer of quality customarily employed by princes or wealthy titled families, and has now come to mean a butler. He was sent to fetch the purest water from the well of St Cuthbert in the grounds, and was astonished to find that fairies were dancing happily round the rim of the well as he drew near. Then he saw that a strange object was half hidden by grass at the foot of the well which, when he snatched it up from the protesting fairies, he found to be a beaker or goblet. As he moved to go the leader of the fairies cried out the warning:

> If that glass either break or fall.
> Farewell the Luck of Eden Hall.

Whether the Musgraves believed in fairies or not, though many people did at that time, the words of warning were certainly heeded and it was jealously preserved by them for some seven centuries, except for one dangerous incident when the warning nearly ended both goblet and family. It happened in the month of September 1721 when the Musgraves were holding a celebration drinking-party at which their principal guest and cousin, the 1st Duke of Wharton, one of whose ancestors was a notable drunkard, suddenly insisted that they should all drink out of the luck. When it came to his turn to drink from that most precious goblet he is said to have drained it and tossed it into the air, though he might well have let it slip from his grasp. It was a most observant butler, familiar with the Duke's capacity for drink, who managed to catch it into his napkin with what was surely outstanding dexterity. Later when the duke was sober he wrote some bad verses on the occasion, two lines of which ran:

> God prosper long from being broke
> The Luck of Eden Hall.

In spite of all the care the Musgrave family took with their luck they must surely have taken another grave risk when they lent it for display at the famous 1862 Exhibition. After the demolition of Eden Hall the precious goblet was in the custody of the Bank of England but was later in 1958 acquired by the Victoria and Albert Museum in London. The baronetcy of the Musgraves is till extant.

THE PENNINGTONS

THE LUCK OF MUNCASTER CASTLE

Muncaster Castle, built between the years 1862 and 1866, is visited annually by many thousands of visitors, for it is renowned for its rhododendrons, its exotic birds and its superb setting and spectacular views. The modern castle incorporates the former ancient peel tower used in medieval times throughout Cumbria for defence against the Scottish invaders. The precious luck of Muncaster was given to Sir John Pennington by Henry VI as a mark of gratitude for giving him shelter after his defeat in the battle of Hexham in 1463, when the half-mad and distressed King was in flight. It is a very beautiful glass bowl of the fifteenth century, possibly of Venetian workmanship, pale violet in colour, decorated with a gold band and white spots of enamel in groups of three and a row of gold billets beneath with a reversed band of purple spots.

The Penningtons and the Musgraves were near kinsmen and neighbours, both of whom were aware of the need for protection of their lucks. The Penningtons have always kept their luck in the castle vaults, though a replica was made for exhibition to visitors to see. Like the Musgraves, the Penningtons' luck had a narrow escape from disaster – in far more perilous circumstances than those brought about by the inebriated Duke.

Lord and Lady Muncaster were with a distinguished party of titled people visiting Athens some time after their marriage in 1863. While they were returning from Marathon they were captured and badly treated by bandits, who took them to their secret hiding-place in the mountains. The date was 11 April. The next day the bandits ordered one of the party to go to Athens, and demand £30,000 in gold, the release of former gang prisoners and safe ransom granted to them; they declared that failure to obey would result in the killing of all the other hostages. Lots were drawn but the winner, who was unmarried, offered his chance to Lord Muncaster who left for Athens two days later. The Greek Government agreed to the terms but sent a private expedition to capture the bandits who, however, found out and shot four of the hostages. The bandits were nevertheless caught and executed in Athens. Lord Muncaster never recovered from the shock but erected a stained-glass window in the church to the memory of those who had been murdered. On a tomb in that same church, as if to commemorate in perpetuity the royal gift of the luck of Muncaster are the inscribed words: 'King Harry gave Syr John a brauve workyd glasse cuppe with his word before yat whyllys the famylie should keep it unbrecken thei shold gretely thrif, and never lack a male heir.'

The family of Pennington continued to thrive, becoming ennobled in 1783 as Baron Muncaster. The luck ran out at last as the last and 5th Baron died in 1917 without an heir. Geoffrey William Pennington, second son of Sir John Ramsden 6th Baronet assumed by deed poll in 1925 the surname of Pennington in lieu of Ramsden in accordance with the will of the late Lord Muncaster.

Bibliography

Andrews, R.T., Moats and Moated Sites of Hertfordshire
Anglo-Saxon Chronicle (1972)
Aubrey, J., *Brief Lives* (Cresset Press, 1949)
Bain, J., *Sir John Robsart and his daughter Amy* (Edinburgh)
Barclay, T.W.C., *The Story of Brent Pelham*
Baring-Gould, S., *Cornish Characters and Strange Events* (1932)
Barron, E.M., *Scottish Wars of Independence* (1934)
Barton, S., *Castles in Britain* (1973)
Bath, Marchioness of, *Longleat*
Bellamy, J.S., *The Law of Treason in England in the Middle Ages* (Cambridge, 1970)
Beroul, *Le Roman de Tristan*
Blind Hary, *Wallace Scottish Text Society* (Edinburgh, 1908/9)
Boutell, C., *Heraldry* (1976)
Bridge, J.C., *Two Cheshire Soldiers* (1907)
Bryant, A., *The Age of Chivalry* (F. Warne and Co., 1950)
Burke, B., *Vicissitudes of Families*
Burke, J. & B., *Peerage*
——, *Extinct and Dormant Peerage*
——, *Landed Gentry*
Burton, N., *Historic Houses Handbook* (RAC, 1981)
Cockayne, G.C., *Complete Peerage*
Coxe, A.D., *Haunted Britain* (1973)
Croslan, *Outlaws in Fact and Fiction* (Owen, 1989)
Debrett, *Baronetage Knightage & Companionage* (London 1892)
Delaney, T., *Six Worthy Yeomen of the West* (Oxford, 1912)
Ditmas, E.R.M., *Tristan and Iseult in Cornwall* (Gloster, 1967)
Dugdale, Sir W., *The Antiquities of Warwickshire* (1665)
du Maurier, D., *Vanishing Cornwall* (Gollancz, 1965)
Durham, MS, Parish of Sockburn
Fox-Davies, A.C. *Complete Guide to Heraldry* (Nelson, 1909)
Fraser, Sir J., *Historic Works* (Everyman)

Geoffrey of Monmouth, *The Kings of Britain* (A. Thompson, 1718)
Gerish, W.B., *A Hertfordshire St. George*
——, *A Tour Through Hertfordshire* (1924)
Gesta Herewardi, *Rolls series* (London, 1889)
Grove, F., *The Antiquities of Scotland* (London 1789/91)
Halliday, F.E., *A History of Cornwall* (Duckworth, 1959)
Hare, K., *Gloucestershire* (Hale)
Harper, C.G., *Haunted Houses* (EP, 1974)
Henderson, C., *Essays in Cornish History*
Henry the Minstrel, *The Life and Deeds of Sir William Wallace*
'Highways and Byways', county series (Macmillan)
Hussey, C., Lambton Castle (Country Life, 1960)
Hutchins, T., *The History of the County of Cumberland* (Carlisle, 1794)
Hutchinson, W., *The History and Antiquities of the County Palatine of Durham* (1794)
Ingram, J.H., *Haunted Houses and Family Traditions of Great Britain* (Allen, 1890)
Jenkin, A.K.H., *Cornwall and its people* (1945)
Jolliffe, J., (ed. & trans.) *Froissart's Chronicles* (Harvill, 1967)
Jones G. and T., (trans.) *The Mabinogion* (Dent, 1949)
Kaye, *Norfolk Families* (1913)
Keen, M.H., *The Outlaws of Medieval History* (London, 1877)
Kightly, C., *Folk Heroes of Britain* (Thames & Hudson, 1984)
Magna Britannia, various counties (London, 1806)
Mann, F.C., *The Worthies of Thomas Delaney* (1912)
Marie de France, *La Folle Tristan* (twelfth century)
Mee, A., 'The King's England (Hodder & Stoughton Ltd, 1938)
Miller, A.C., *Sir Henry Killigrew* (Leicester, 1963)
Morris, J.E., *The Welsh Wars of Edward I* (Edinburgh)
Murray's Guides', various counties (John Murray)
Ormerod, G., *The history of Cheshire*
Poole, K.B., *Historic Heraldic Families* (David & Charles, 1975)
——, *Ghosts of Wessex* (David & Charles 1976)
Reader's Digest, *Folk Lore Myths and Legends of Britain* (Reader's Digest, 1973)
Roby, J., *Traditions of Lancashire* (1829/31)
Rye, W., Norfolk Families (Norwich, 1913)
Scott, Sir W., *Kenilworth* (Ward Lock)
Sorrell, H., *Living history of Scotland* (1969)
Stow, J., *Survey of London* (Everyman)
Stuart & Paul, *Scottish Family History* (Edinburgh, 1936)
Summers, W.H., *The story of Hungerford*

Surtees, R., *History and antiquities of the County Palatine of Durham*
Taylor, J., *Great historic families of Scotland* (London, 1887)
Trevelyan, G.M., *Shortened History of England* (Penguin, 1931)
——, *English Social history* (Longman, 1945)
Tyler, P., *History of Scotland* (Edinburgh, 1867)
'Victoria County History', various counties
Waller, A.K., *Cambridge History of English Literature* (Cambridge, 1940)
Westcott, E.T., *A View of Devonshire with Pedigrees of the Gentry* (1650)
Westwood, J., *Albion* (Grafton, 1987)
Williams, E.C., *Companion into Oxfordshire* (Hale, 1951)
Yarrow, I., *Berkshire* (Hale, 1952)

OTHER SOURCES

Local historical societies; *Dictionary of National Biography*; regional journals and newspapers; documents from various libraries, field clubs and magazines; *Newbury News* Round the Villages series; stately home guides; and considerable research into pedigrees of families, their traditions and events in their history and homes.

Index